Ultimate Certified FinOps Practitioner Exam Guide

Master Cloud Financial Operations with Real-World Strategies, Hands-On Tools, and Complete Preparation for the Certified FinOps Practitioner Exam

Raphael Gab-Momoh

www.orangeava.com

First Published: November 2025

Published By: Orange Education Pvt Ltd, AVA®

Address: 9, Daryaganj, Delhi, 110002, India

275 New North Road Islington Suite 1314 London,
N1 7AA, United Kingdom

ISBN (PBK): 978-93-49888-97-5

ISBN (E-BOOK): 978-93-49888-94-4

Scan the QR code to explore our entire catalogue

www.orangeava.com

Dedicated To

My Mother

And

Everyone out there who is trying to be the best version of themselves everyday.

About the Author

Raphael Gab-Momoh is a seasoned Cloud and FinOps Engineer with over a decade of experience in cloud architecture, cost optimization, and financial operations. A recognized leader in the tech community, he holds the prestigious Microsoft Most Valuable Professional (MVP) award and is a FinOps Certified Professional, Practitioner, and Focus Analyst.

His expertise spans major cloud platforms – AWS, Azure, Google Cloud, Oracle Cloud Infrastructure, and Nutanix – and he is proficient in automation tools such as Terraform, Ansible, Kubernetes, and Jenkins, as well as programming languages including Python, Bash, and SQL.

Raphael holds a Bachelor's in Information Systems from Middlesex University and a Diploma in Electronic Engineering from Swinburne University of Technology. He is currently pursuing a Master's in Financial Engineering at WorldQuant University, blending technical depth with financial acumen.

His certifications include:

- FinOps Certified Professional, Practitioner, Focus Analyst
- Microsoft Azure Architect Expert, Developer Associate
- Google Cloud Associate Cloud Engineer
- Google Cloud Professional Cloud Architect
- Google Cloud Machine Learning Engineer
- Google Cloud Professional DevOps Engineer
- Oracle Cloud Infrastructure Certified
- AWS Solutions Architect Professional
- Nutanix Certified Professional
- Certified Kubernetes Administrator (CKA)

Raphael's mission is to help organizations maximize ROI on their cloud investments through data-driven strategies, automation, and cross-functional collaboration.

About the Technical Reviewer

Dieter Matzion is a member of Roku's Cloud Technology and Infrastructure team, supporting Cloud FinOps across AWS, GCP, and Azure. Recently, Dieter was a part of Intuit's Technology Finance team, where he supported the AWS cost optimization program. Prior to Intuit, Dieter worked on Netflix's AWS capacity team, contributing to the development of Netflix's rhythm and active management of AWS. Before Netflix, Dieter spent two years at Google, focusing on capacity planning and resource provisioning for the Google Cloud offering.

During his time at Google, he developed demand-planning models and automation tools for capacity management. Originally a native from Germany, Dieter holds an M.S. in computer science. Outside his profession, Dieter prioritizes spending time with his family, and enjoying outdoor activities such as hiking, camping, horseback riding, and cave exploration.

Acknowledgments

Writing this book has been both a professional milestone and a deeply personal journey – one shaped by years of experience, continuous learning, and the support of an incredible community.

I am deeply grateful to the FinOps Foundation and its global network of practitioners. Your vision for financial accountability in the cloud has redefined how organizations manage their cloud investments, and your open, collaborative culture has directly influenced the philosophy and structure of this guide.

Special thanks to my mentors and peers in the Microsoft MVP and AWS Community Builder programs. Your technical insights, encouragement, and shared experiences have been invaluable in shaping not only this book, but my own professional path. I'm also thankful to the engineering, finance, and operations teams I've worked with over the years – your real-world challenges and successes have informed every practical example and case study in this book.

I extend my appreciation to the technical reviewers and contributors who helped validate concepts, refine explanations, and ensure accuracy across platforms like AWS, Azure, and Google Cloud. Your feedback ensures this guide remains both technically rigorous and accessible.

To my family, thank you for your patience, understanding, and endless encouragement during the long nights and weekends spent writing, researching, and revising. This achievement is as much yours as it is mine.

To someone I deeply admire- You are one of the most courageous people I've ever known, not because life has been easy, but because you keep choosing to move forward, to believe in change, and to build a better future for yourself. That kind of strength is rare

I've always dreamed of sharing my adventures with someone who sees travel not just as escape, but as growth and new beginnings. The fact that you've said yes to joining me on these journeys means more than I can say. It's not just about the places we go, but about the trust, the conversations, and the quiet belief that we're both becoming better versions of ourselves. Thank you for your openness, your faith, and your courage

Finally, to you, the reader – thank you for investing your time and energy into mastering FinOps. Whether you're preparing for certification or aiming to drive change in your organization, I hope this guide becomes a trusted companion on your journey to growth, impact, and success.

Preface

Cloud computing has transformed the way businesses innovate, scale, and deliver value. But with this transformation comes a new challenge: how do we manage costs in an environment where resources are elastic, usage is dynamic, and spending can spiral out of control in minutes?

Enter FinOps – the cultural and operational discipline that brings financial accountability to cloud spending without sacrificing speed, agility, or innovation.

This book, *Ultimate Certified FinOps Practitioner Exam Guide*, is designed to be your definitive companion in mastering the FinOps framework and preparing for the Certified FinOps Practitioner exam. Whether you're a cloud engineer, DevOps specialist, financial analyst, or IT leader, this guide will equip you with the knowledge, tools, and practical strategies to take control of cloud costs and drive meaningful financial optimization.

The book is structured around the FinOps lifecycle – Inform, Optimize, and Operate – providing a clear, actionable roadmap for implementing FinOps in any organization. You'll learn how to:

- Gain visibility into cloud spending using tagging, allocation models, and reporting tools
- Optimize costs through rightsizing, reserved instances, spot usage, and workload scheduling
- Embed cost governance into daily operations and team workflows
- Leverage powerful tools like AWS Cost Explorer, Azure Cost Management, GCP Billing, CloudHealth, Apptio Cloudability, and CloudCheckr
- Prepare confidently for the FinOps certification with practice questions, mock exams, and exam tips

Each chapter includes hands-on exercises, real-world case studies, and actionable insights drawn from my experience as a Microsoft MVP, FinOps Certified Professional, and cloud practitioner with over a decade in IT.

This book is not just about passing an exam – it's about building a mindset. FinOps is not a one-time project; it's a continuous journey of collaboration, visibility, and improvement across engineering, finance, and business teams.

If you're ready to take control of cloud costs, align technology with business goals, and position yourself as a leader in one of the fastest-growing domains in tech – this book is for you.

Let's begin.

Get a Free eBook

We hope you are enjoying your recently purchased book! Your feedback is incredibly valuable to us, and to all other readers looking for great books.

If you found this book helpful or enjoyable, we would truly appreciate it, if you could take a moment to leave a short review with a 5 star rating on Amazon. It helps us grow, and lets other readers discover our books.

As a thank you, we would love to send you a free digital copy of this book, and a **30%** discount code on your next cart value on our official websites:

www.orangeava.com

www.orangeava.in (For Indian Subcontinent)

☑ **Here's how:**

Leave a review for the book on Amazon.

Take a screenshot of your review, and send an email to **info@orangeava.com** (it can be just the confirmation screen).

Once, we receive your screenshot, we will send you the digital file, within 24 hours.

Thank you so much for your support – it means a lot to us!

Downloading the code bundles and colored images

Please follow the links or scan the QR codes to download the **_Code Bundles and Images_** of the book:

https://github.com/ava-orange-education/Ultimate-Certified-FinOps-Practitioner-Exam-Guide

The code bundles and images of the book are also hosted on **_https://rebrand.ly/be0697_**

In case there's an update to the code, it will be updated on the existing GitHub repository.

Errata

We take immense pride in our work at **Orange Education Pvt Ltd,** and follow best practices to ensure the accuracy of our content to provide an indulging reading experience to our subscribers. Our readers are our mirrors, and we use their inputs to reflect and improve upon human errors, if any, that may have occurred during the publishing processes involved. To let us maintain the quality and help us reach out to any readers who might be having difficulties due to any unforeseen errors, please write to us at :

errata@orangeava.com

Your support, suggestions, and feedback are highly appreciated.

DID YOU KNOW

Did you know that Orange Education Pvt Ltd offers eBook versions of every book published, with PDF and ePub files available? You can upgrade to the eBook version at **www.orangeava.com** and as a print book customer, you are entitled to a discount on the eBook copy. Get in touch with us at: **info@orangeava.com** for more details.

At **www.orangeava.com**, you can also read a collection of free technical articles, sign up for a range of free newsletters, and receive exclusive discounts and offers on Print Books and eBooks.

PIRACY

If you come across any illegal copies of our works in any form on the internet, we would be grateful if you would provide us with the location address or website name. Please contact us at **info@orangeava.com** with a link to the material.

ARE YOU INTERESTED IN AUTHORING WITH US?

If there is a topic that you have expertise in, and you are interested in either writing or contributing to a book, please write to us at **business@orangeava.com**. We are on a journey to help developers and tech professionals to gain insights on the present technological advancements and innovations happening across the globe and build a community that believes Knowledge is best acquired by sharing and learning with others. Please reach out to us to learn what our audience demands and how you can be part of this educational reform. We also welcome ideas from tech experts and help them build learning and development content for their domains.

REVIEWS

Please leave a review. Once you have read and used this book, why not leave a review on the site that you purchased it from? Potential readers can then see and use your unbiased opinion to make purchase decisions. We at Orange Education would love to know what you think about our products, and our authors can learn from your feedback. Thank you!

For more information about Orange Education, please visit **www.orangeava.com**.

Table of Contents

CHAPTER 1
The Rise of FinOps

Introduction

Imagine that your company has embraced the cloud, expecting to save money and boost efficiency. But instead of cost savings, you are staring at a cloud bill that keeps escalating. You might wonder about what went wrong. More often than not, the culprit is not the cloud itself, but a lack of financial governance. Without clear accountability and visibility into spending, cloud costs can spiral out of control. This scenario is way more common than you might expect and is one of the main reasons why FinOps is so important.

FinOps, which stands for Financial Operations, is a transformative approach to managing cloud spending instead of being a buzzword. It brings together finance, IT, and business teams to create a culture of accountability, transparency, and collaboration on optimizing cloud costs. In this chapter, we will explore how FinOps came to be, why it matters, and how it helps organizations get the most out of their cloud investments.

Structure

In this chapter, the topics to be covered are as follows:

- Definition and origins of FinOps
- Importance of cloud financial accountability
- Impact of FinOps on business and cloud adoption strategies
- FinOps Teams, Motivation, and Culture

Defining FinOps

According to the FinOps Foundation, FinOps is an operational framework and cultural practice that maximizes the business value of cloud and technology. As a result, it enables users to make data-driven decisions on time and creates financial accountability by forging collaboration between engineering, finance, and business teams. At its core, FinOps is about making smarter decisions while focusing on cloud spending. Instead of merely cutting costs, it ensures that every dollar spent on the cloud delivers a measurable value. FinOps acts as a bridge between technical delivery and financial stewardship, thereby aligning the goals of engineering teams that focus on innovation and performance with those of finance teams, that prioritize controlling costs and maintaining efficiency.

Origins of FinOps: From Chaos to Control

In the early days of cloud computing, businesses were captivated by its promises of infinite scalability, instant provisioning, and incurring lower upfront costs. For many organizations, migrating to the cloud felt like stepping into the future. But as companies embraced this new change, they quickly encountered the unexpected challenge of confronting unpredictable costs.

This was the case for a mid-sized tech startup in 2013. Its engineering team was thrilled to spin up servers for testing, deploy applications faster than ever, and scale resources on demand. Yet, when their first cloud bill arrived, it was double of what they had anticipated. The finance department scrambled to make sense of line items labeled "EC2 (Elastic Compute Cloud) Instances," "S3 (Simple Storage Service) Buckets," and "Data Transfer Out." The challenge unfolded as engineers shrugged off the concerns saying, "It is just how the cloud works."

This glaring incompatibility between technical agility and financial accountability became a recurring theme across industries. By 2015, the problem had grown so acute that CFOs began demanding answers about where cloud costs were spiraling out of control, who was responsible for managing them, and how organizations could regain control without stifling innovation.

The Birth of FinOps

This was what led to the entry of FinOps, which was a term coined by industry pioneers J.R. Storment and Mike Fuller in their influential 2017 whitepaper, *Controlling Cloud Costs.*[1] FinOps did not just cut costs, it also created a cultural shift. The concept introduced the idea that cloud spending should be treated as a shared responsibility, where finance, IT, and business[1] teams worked together to align costs with value.

At its core, FinOps is built on three pillars: visibility, accountability, and optimization. These principles emerged from the chaos of early cloud adoption and have since

[1] J.R. Storment and Mike Fuller, *Controlling Cloud Costs*, 2017 – this paper is widely credited with coining the term "FinOps" and laying the foundation for cloud financial management as a collaborative, cross-functional discipline.

become the foundation of modern cloud financial management in the following ways:

- **Visibility:** Before the emergence of FinOps, cloud spending was often a black box. Teams would provision resources without understanding their financial impact, which often led to wasted budgets and unused assets. FinOps introduced tools such as tagging, dashboards, and real-time cost tracking to make cloud spending more transparent. For example, a global e-commerce company preparing for Black Friday sales can tag resources by environment such as, Production vs. Testing, to identify cost-intensive workloads and allocate budgets accordingly. This level of visibility not only reduces waste but also empowers teams to make smarter decisions.
- **Accountability:** One of the biggest challenges in cloud cost management is assigning ownership. In traditional IT setups, finance teams handled budgets while engineers focused on delivering solutions. FinOps broke down these silos by introducing the concept of "cost ownership." Take Netflix, for instance. As one of the earliest adopters of cloud-native architectures, Netflix faced significant challenges in managing AWS costs. To address this, the company implemented a policy where every product team was responsible for the costs associated with their features. If a team launched a new recommendation algorithm, it also owned up to corresponding cloud expenses. The approach fostered a culture of accountability, ensuring that every dollar spent delivered a measurable value.
- **Optimization:** Finally, FinOps emphasizes continuous improvement through practices such as right-sizing, automation, and lifecycle management. Rightsizing involves adjusting resource allocations to match the actual usage, while automation eliminates manual inefficiencies. Lifecycle management ensures that unused or underutilized resources are decommissioned promptly. A notable example is Dropbox, which saved $10 million annually by optimizing its AWS infrastructure. The company identified two major culprits: overprovisioned instances and stale data stored in S3 buckets. By right-sizing servers and deleting redundant files, Dropbox reduced waste without compromising its performance.

The Evolution of FinOps

As more organizations adopted FinOps, the discipline evolved beyond cost management and went on to encompass broader strategic goals. Companies began using FinOps to drive innovation, improve sustainability, and enhance customer experience.

For instance, organizations have recognized the importance of FinOps not only for cost optimization but also for strategic outcomes like sustainability and operational efficiency. By leveraging FinOps practices, many companies have been able to identify and eliminate idle cloud resources and have reduced unnecessary energy consumption while supporting broader environmental goals.

Today, FinOps has become a cornerstone of modern cloud operations. The FinOps Foundation, launched in 2020, provides certifications, a list of best practices, and community support to assist organizations in implementing FinOps at scale. According to the *Flexera 2023 State of the Cloud Report*, managing cloud spending is the foremost challenge for organizations around the globe.[2] Although 72% of these enterprises are using FinOps tools, the opportunity to improve cost optimization across the board remains untapped.

Looking Ahead

The rise of FinOps marks a pivotal moment in the evolution of cloud financial management. What began as a response to chaotic billing has grown into a transformative discipline that bridges technology, finance, and strategy. As cloud ecosystems continue to expand, with advancements in edge computing, AI, and IoT, the importance of FinOps will only increase in the future.

Organizations that embrace FinOps today will be able to navigate upcoming complexities more efficiently. By fostering collaboration, embracing transparency, and prioritizing value, they can turn cloud costs from a liability into a strategic asset.

In the words of a senior FinOps practitioner: "The cloud is not free—but with FinOps, it does not have to be wasteful."[3]

Visual Summary Table

The following table highlights the key difference between Traditional IT Costs (Fixed) versus Cloud Costs (Variable). Traditional IT costs are predictable, while Cloud Costs are variable and prone to surprises. FinOps helps organizations navigate this shift.

---

[2] Flexera, *Cloud Computing Trends: Flexera 2023 State of the Cloud Report*, https://www.flexera.com/blog/finops/cloud-computing-trends-flexera-2023-state-of-the-cloud-report/

[3] This quote echoes a key insight from the Flexera 2023 State of the Cloud Report: managing cloud spend is now the top challenge, making FinOps essential for cost optimization and strategic cloud management. *Source*: Flexera Blog – 2023 State of the Cloud Report

	Traditional IT Cost Management	FinOps Approach
Cost Structure	Fixed costs (e.g., hardware purchases, maintenance contracts)	Vanable costs (e.g., on-demand resources, pay-as-you-go pricing
Predictability	Predictable spending patterns	Unpredictable spending due to dynamic usage
Flexibility	Limited flexibility in scaling resources	High flexibility in scaling resour- up or down as needed
Resource Allocation	Static allocation based on upfront planning	Dynamic allocation based on real-time demand
Optimization Focus	Centralized financial control by IT teams	Shared responsibility across finance, IT, and business teams
Otimizastion Focus	Focus on minimizing upfront capital expenditures	Focus on optimizing cloud spend while aligning with busine
Visibility	Limited visibility into cost drivers	Comprehensive visibility into cloud usage and costs
Decision-Making	Reactive decision-making based on fixed budgets	Proactive decision-making drive en by dat and collaboration

Figure 1.1: *Traditional IT Costs (Fixed) versus Cloud Costs (Variable)*

The Value of FinOps: Driving Accountability and Transparency for Cloud Spending

Imagine entering an office where every employee has access to the company credit card, but no one tracks how much they spend. Lunches are charged to the company account, subscriptions pile up, and receipts vanish. By the end of the month, the leadership is scratching their heads over a bloated bill.

Now, replace that credit card with cloud resources. Developers spin up servers for testing, storage buckets overflow with unused data, and reserved instances sit idle. Without oversight, this unchecked spending can spiral out of control, just like the aforementioned example of unmonitored credit card expenses.

This is where FinOps steps in. It transforms chaotic cloud spending into a disciplined practice by introducing two critical elements: accountability and transparency. Together, these principles ensure that every dollar spent delivers measurable value to the business.

Assigning Cloud Cost Ownership

In traditional IT setups, finance teams handle budgets while engineers focus on delivering solutions. But the cloud blurs these lines. Engineers provision resources, often without considering their financial impact. Meanwhile, finance teams struggle to decode complex invoices filled with cryptic terms such as “EC2 Instances” or “Data Transfer Out.”

FinOps bridges this gap by fostering a culture of shared responsibility. It assigns ownership of cloud costs to the teams driving consumption. This shift does not mean engineers need to become accountants–it means they need to think critically about the financial implications of their decisions.

Netflix provides a striking example of how accountability can shape cloud efficiency. In its early transition to cloud-native operations, the company noticed that AWS costs were spiraling without clear ownership. Rather than centralizing control, Netflix pushed responsibility to the edges: every product team became answerable for the cloud usage of its own features. So when engineers built a new recommendation system, they also managed the financial footprint that came with it.

This approach had several benefits, which are listed as follows:

- **Empowerment:** Teams became more mindful of resource usage, knowing they would be held accountable for overspending.
- **Collaboration:** Finance and engineering teams began working together to align budgets with technical requirements.
- **Innovation:** By tying costs to outcomes, Netflix ensured that every dollar spent contributed to customer satisfaction and business growth.

[This aligns with Exam Objective 3: Financial Accountability, which emphasizes cost ownership and cross-team collaboration. It reflects the importance of embedding financial awareness into technical workflows–key knowledge for FinOps practitioners.]

Transparency: Shining a Light on Cloud Costs

One of the biggest hurdles in cloud spending is knowing about where the money is going. Without clear visibility of expenses, it is easy to lose track of costs across departments, projects, or environments. A single invoice might include charges for marketing campaigns, production servers, and development environments and can lump them together.

FinOps solves this problem by providing tools and practices to track real-time spending. Here are how transparency transforms cloud operations:

- **Tagging Resources:** Tagging is like labeling items in a grocery store. It categorizes the cloud resources so that you know about what you are paying for. For example:
    - A retail company might tag resources by department (for example, marketing) or environment (for example, production).
    - A SaaS provider can use tags to differentiate between customer-facing applications and internal tools.

    This level of granularity enables teams to allocate budgets accurately and identify areas for improvement.

- **Real-Time Dashboards:** Tools such as AWS Cost Explorer, Azure Cost Management, and third-party platforms provide dashboards that display real-time spending trends. These visualizations make it easier to spot anomalies, such as sudden spikes in usage or unexpected charges.

    Consider Capital One, which uses tagging and dashboards to calculate "cost per customer." By understanding how much each subscriber contributes to cloud expenses, the company can optimize spending while scaling its user base.

- **Detailed Reporting:** Generating reports allows organizations to delve into specific areas of concern. For instance:
    - A SaaS provider might analyze storage configurations to identify inefficient setups.
    - An e-commerce company could review compute usage during peak sales periods to ensure resources are scaled appropriately.

    These insights empower teams to make data-driven decisions, while reducing wastage of resources.

[This aligns with Exam Objective 2: Cloud Cost Visibility, which focuses on enabling financial transparency through tagging, dashboards, and reporting. These are effectively essential skills for tracking and managing cloud spend.]

Case Study: Dropbox's $10 Million Savings

The journey of Dropbox highlights the power of transparency. The company's FinOps team identified two major issues:

- **Overprovisioned Instances**: 30% of AWS servers were larger than needed
- **Zombie Assets**: 200TB of stale data sat unused in S3 buckets

By implementing strong FinOps practices such as resource tagging, automated cleanup, and rightsizing, companies can uncover hidden inefficiencies. In Dropbox's case, this approach reportedly saved millions of dollars, which were reinvested into product innovation. The incident demonstrated how cost transparency can drive business growth and agility.[2]

The Ripple Effect of Accountability and Transparency

When accountability and transparency are embedded into cloud operations, the benefits extend far beyond cost savings and lead to the following:

- **Improved Collaboration:** Breaking down silos between finance, engineering, and leadership fosters trust and alignment as teams work together[4] to balance innovation with fiscal discipline
- **Faster Decision-Making:** Real-time visibility enables organizations to respond quickly to changing market conditions. For example, an e-commerce company can scale resources dynamically during Black Friday sales without overspending
- **Sustainability Goals:** Reducing cloud waste is not just economical–it is ecological. A single unused server emits 2.5 tons of CO_2 annually. By optimizing resources, companies like Etsy have cut energy consumption by 15% to support their net-zero pledge

Turning Chaos into Clarity

Cloud spending does not have to be a mystery or a liability. With FinOps, organizations can introduce accountability and transparency into their operations and ensure that every dollar spent delivers measurable value.

As one FinOps practitioner put it: "It is not about cutting corners–it is about creating clarity. When teams understand the financial impact of their actions, they make smarter choices."

By embracing these principles, businesses can unlock the full potential of the cloud as they drive innovation, enhance efficiency, and achieve sustainable growth.

[4] "Reduce Cloud Costs: Watch Out for Zombie Instances." *Flexera Blog*, 2023. https://www.flexera.com/blog/finops/reduce-cloud-costs-watch-out-for-zombie-instances

The Impact of FinOps on Business: Aligning Spending with Strategic Goals

FinOps is not just about saving money, but ensuring that every amount spent on the cloud contributes to the organization's success. One may think of it as strategic financial stewardship, where cloud investments are aligned with business objectives, rather than being a mere afterthought.

For example:

- A retail company might allocate cloud resources to handle peak holiday traffic, contributing to a seamless customer experience during critical sales periods such as Black Friday or Cyber Monday.
- A software-as-a-service (SaaS) provider might optimize cloud costs to offer competitive pricing while maintaining profitability, enabling them to scale without sacrificing margins.

Organizations can turn their cloud investments into a competitive advantage by tying cloud spending to strategic goals. Let us explore how FinOps achieves this through three key areas: aligning spending with strategy, enhancing agility, and promoting scalability and efficiency.

Aligning Spending with Strategic Goals

In today's fast-paced business environment, companies must ensure that their cloud spending supports broader organizational objectives. Without alignment, cloud costs can spiral out of control and divert funds from high-priority initiatives.

Case Study: Retail Giant Optimizes Holiday Traffic

During every holiday season, a global e-commerce retailer faced the same dilemma: either risk crashing its servers during traffic spikes, or overspend on infrastructure that sat idle once the rush was over. Both options drove up costs and reduced **profitability**, ultimately affecting the customer experience.

To solve this, they leaned into FinOps. By tagging resources based on campaigns like "Black Friday Promo" and using predictive analytics and real-time monitoring, they could automatically scale their infrastructure up or down as needed. This approach ensured that their site remained fast and reliable during peak shopping times without burning through their budget. In the end, they not only delivered a smoother customer experience but also cut cloud waste by 25%.

This example reflects real-world strategies used by leading e-commerce companies, as reported in cloud cost optimization case studies such as those published by Hystax.

Example: SaaS Provider Balances Pricing and Profitability

A mid-sized SaaS provider faced a similar challenge. Their product was gaining traction, but rising cloud costs threatened profitability. To stay competitive, they needed to keep the subscription fees low while ensuring reliable service.

Using FinOps principles, the company identified inefficiencies like idle instances and overprovisioned databases. They implemented rightsizing strategies and negotiated reserved instance discounts with their cloud provider. These changes allowed them to cut costs by 30% and freed up capital that was invested in new features and customer support.

Therefore, by aligning cloud spending with strategic goals, businesses can achieve both short-term wins and long-term sustainability.[5]

Enhancing Agility: Responding to Market Changes

Flexibility, if managed effectively, is one of the biggest advantages of the. FinOps enables organizations to respond quickly to changing market conditions by providing real-time visibility and predictive analytics.

For instance, a startup launches a new mobile app. However, initial user adoption exceeds expectations and traffic spikes overnight. Without FinOps, the company might struggle to scale resources efficiently, risking downtime or overspending.

With FinOps, however, the team has access to dashboards showing real-time cost trends and usage patterns. Predictive analytics forecast future demand, enabling proactive adjustments. For instance:

- If traffic surges unexpectedly, auto-scaling policies kick in to provision additional servers.
- When demand dips, unused resources are automatically decommissioned to avoid unnecessary charges.

---

[5] *This is based on a case study by Ataiva, where a comparable mid-sized SaaS operation achieved a 15% reduction in cloud costs through rightsizing, waste elimination, and reserved instance commitments. Link: https://ativa.com/case-study-cutting-cloud-costs-by-30-percent/*

This level of agility allows teams to innovate faster while maintaining fiscal discipline.

Real-World Example: E-Commerce Platform Adapts to Pandemic Demand

During the COVID-19 pandemic, a rapidly growing e-commerce platform faced escalating cloud costs as demand surged. To maintain performance without overspending, the company adopted FinOps practices to manage growth efficiently. They implemented comprehensive resource tagging by region and leveraged monitoring tools like CloudCheckr to analyze usage trends. This allowed them to identify where capacity was truly needed and where resources could be safely decommissioned. Through rightsizing over 200 EC2 instances and eliminating redundancies, the company achieved a 42% reduction in monthly AWS costs—while continuing to deliver a seamless customer experience.[6]

Scalability and Efficiency: Doing More with Less

As businesses grow, so do their cloud requirements. However, scaling without oversight can lead to inefficiencies and runaway costs. FinOps promotes the efficient use of cloud resources, ensuring that organizations scale responsibly.

Key Practices for Scalability and Efficiency

- **Rightsizing Resources**: Adjusting instance sizes to match actual usage.
- **Lifecycle Management**: Decommissioning unused or underutilized resources promptly.
- **Automation**: Using scripts and tools to streamline repetitive tasks such as cost monitoring and cleanup.

Case Study: Netflix Achieves 30% Cost Reduction

During its rapid growth, Netflix faced the challenge of managing a massive and ever-scaling cloud infrastructure on AWS to support hundreds of millions of global users. To keep its costs in check without compromising performance, Netflix embraced FinOps principles. The company developed internal tools like **Scryer** to

[6] "Cloud Cost Optimisation Strategies." *Precision* IT, 2023. https://precisionit.com.au/cloud-cost-optimization-strategies

forecast demand spikes and automatically adjust compute resources in real time. It also utilized **reserved instances** for steady workloads and created a system that repurposed unused capacity for tasks like video encoding.

These efforts paid off. Netflix reportedly reduced its cloud costs by 25-30% while maintaining exceptional streaming quality. More importantly, the savings were reinvested into product innovation, which included personalized recommendations and interactive content, thereby helping the company stay ahead in a fiercely competitive market.[7]

[This aligns with Exam Objective 5: Continuous Optimization, which emphasizes the use of automation, forecasting, and iterative improvements to maximize cloud value. These are essential skills for FinOps practitioners who are focused on long-term cost efficiency and innovation.]

The Ripple Effect of FinOps

When organizations embrace FinOps, the benefits extend far beyond cost savings:

- **Strategic Alignment**: Cloud spending supports business objectives and drives growth and innovation.
- **Agility**: Teams can pivot quickly in response to market changes while staying ahead of competitors.
- **Sustainability**: Reducing cloud waste lowers energy consumption and contributes to environmental goals.

Example: Etsy's Sustainability Success

Etsy, a leader in sustainable e-commerce, leveraged FinOps to reduce its carbon footprint. By identifying and eliminating idle cloud resources, the company cut down its energy consumption by 15%, which aligned with its net-zero emissions pledge.

Turning Cloud Costs into Strategic Assets

The impact of FinOps on businesses is profound as it transforms cloud spending into a strategic asset from a liability, and empowers organizations to:

- Align spending with goals and ensuring that every dollar delivers value
- Enhance agility to respond swiftly to market changes

[7] Netflix's FinOps approach, which included predictive scaling through internal tools like Scryer and optimization of reserved capacity, reduced cloud costs by up to 30%. These insights are shared by Netflix engineers and FinOps practitioners like Suyash Salvi on LinkedIn and discussions on r/aws.

- Scale responsibly and maximize efficiency without compromising performance

According to the FinOps Foundation (2023), the goal of FinOps is not merely to reduce cloud costs but to align financial accountability with innovation—empowering teams to make informed trade-offs between speed, quality, and expense.

By embracing FinOps, businesses can navigate the complexities of the digital age with confidence and achieve both financial and operational excellence.

FinOps Teams, Motivation, and Culture: Building the Foundation for Success

Behind every successful FinOps initiative is a team of dedicated individuals working together to align cloud spending with business value. But building effective FinOps practices is not just about assembling the right people, but fostering a larger culture of motivation, collaboration, and a shared commitment towards continuous improvement. Let us explore how organizations can create a strong foundation for FinOps success by understanding who is involved, what drives them, and how to cultivate a culture that supports their efforts:

The Power of Cross-Functional Collaboration

FinOps thrives on diversity, both in thought and in roles. A successful FinOps team brings together professionals from different disciplines, where each contributes their unique expertise to tackle the complexities of cloud financial management. These teams are not siloed; they are interconnected and work as a cohesive unit to ensure that every dollar spent delivers a measurable value. Here is a closer look at the key players:

- **The Executive:** Setting the Vision at the helm is the Executive, who is often a C-level leader such as the CFO, CTO, or CIO. This person champions the FinOps initiative by securing executive buy-in and ensuring that the strategy aligns with broader organizational goals. The Executive is like the captain of a ship. They set the course, allocate resources, and keep everyone focused on the destination. For example, when a leading North American e-commerce retailer began to see sharp increases in its cloud spending during major sales events such as Black Friday and Cyber Monday, the Chief Financial Officer partnered with engineering leaders to implement a FinOps framework. By introducing cost-visibility tools and setting shared accountability for cloud usage across teams, the company reduced unnecessary compute spending, saving several million dollars annually while maintaining a seamless customer experience.

- **The Cloud Engineer:** When it comes to optimizing resources, cloud engineers are the technical backbone of FinOps. These experts design, deploy, and manage cloud infrastructure to make it run efficiently, while saving costs. The role of cloud engineers has evolved with FinOps. Instead of simply provisioning resources, they also think critically about cost implications. For instance, a cloud engineer might identify that a database cluster is over-provisioned and recommends downsizing it to save costs without impacting performance. Tools such as tagging, rightsizing, and automation are part of the engineers' daily toolkit.

  Example: At Spotify, cloud engineers embraced FinOps by tagging Kubernetes clusters and integrating cost data into sprint reviews. Within a year, they reduced waste by 35%, proving that small changes in behavior can lead to significant savings.

- **The Financial Analyst:** Financial analysts act as the bridge between the technical and fiscal worlds. They track spending, analyze trends, and provide budgetary guidance, translating complex cloud invoices into actionable insights. For example, consider that a financial analyst at a noted company notices a sudden spike in storage costs. Upon investigation, they discover that redundant backups are consuming unnecessary space. When the analyst collaborates with the engineers to delete old files, the company saves thousands of dollars monthly.

- **The Business Strategist:** Business strategists ensure that cloud investments support organizational objectives. They ask all the big-picture questions: *How does this cloud spend drive innovation? Are we investing in the right areas to fuel growth?* For example, a SaaS provider's business strategist might evaluate whether a new feature justifies the additional compute costs. By tying spending to strategic outcomes, they ensure every penny contributes to long-term success.

- **The Product Owner:** Product owners bridge the gap between technical teams and business stakeholders. They prioritize features and services based on ROI, ensuring that cloud spending aligns with product goals.

[This aligns with Exam Objective 6: People and Culture, which emphasizes cross-functional collaboration, role clarity, and building a culture of shared accountability. The mentioned principles are key components of a mature FinOps practice.]

Case Study

A retail company's product owner used FinOps dashboards to track the cost per transaction for their e-commerce platform. When they noticed inefficiencies in database queries, they worked with engineers to optimize performance. This reduced costs and improved the user experience, thereby driving higher conversion rates.

Motivation

What motivates FinOps teams to go above and beyond? The answer lies in their ability to deliver tangible benefits to the organization. Here is why these professionals are so passionate about their work:

- **Driving Business Success:** FinOps teams take pride in contributing to the bottom line. Whether it is reducing waste, improving efficiency, or enhancing transparency, their efforts directly influence profitability and growth.
- **Continuous Learning:** The dynamic nature of cloud environments provides endless opportunities for learning and innovation. From mastering new tools to experimenting with optimization strategies, FinOps professionals are constantly improving their skills.
- **Problem-Solving:** Cloud cost management is a puzzle waiting to be solved. Every challenge–whether it is identifying zombie assets or optimizing reserved instances–offers a chance to think creatively and make a difference.
- **Recognition and Impact:** When FinOps teams achieve measurable results, they are often celebrated within the organization. For example, a team that saves $1 million annually might be recognized at company-wide meetings, reinforcing their sense of purpose and accomplishment.

  According to J.R. Storment, Executive Director of the FinOps Foundation, "Every dollar saved is a dollar that can be reinvested into innovation."

Building a Strong FinOps Culture: Collaboration, Accountability, and Continuous Improvement

A strong FinOps culture does not unfold overnight, it requires intentional effort and commitment from everyone in the organization. Here is how companies can cultivate a culture that can support FinOps principles.

- **Open Communication:** Break down silos between departments by fostering open dialogue. Regular meetings, shared dashboards, and using collaborative tools ensure that everyone has access to the same information
- **Shared Accountability:** Assign ownership of cloud costs to the teams driving consumption. For example, if a marketing team launches a campaign using cloud resources, it should also own up to the associated expenses. This approach encourages mindful spending and fosters a sense of responsibility
- **Encouraging Experimentation:** Innovation thrives in environments where failure is seen as a learning opportunity. Encourage teams to experiment with

new tools, strategies, and workflows—even if it means not succeeding every time

- **Celebrating Wins:** Recognize and reward achievements in cost optimization. Whether it is a small win like deleting unused storage, or a major milestone such as reducing cloud costs by 20%, celebrating successes reinforces positive behaviors

Case Study: Adobe's Cultural Transformation

Adobe's strategy to adopt FinOps was not just about saving money, but transforming the way teams worked together. By prioritizing open communication and shared accountability, the company created a culture where engineers, finance professionals, and business leaders collaborate seamlessly. The key outcomes of this strategy were:

- A 25% reduction in cloud costs through rightsizing and automation
- Enhanced collaboration between engineering and finance teams, leading to faster decision-making

Conclusion

The emergence of FinOps is a significant moment in the evolution of cloud financial management. By addressing the challenges associated with cloud spending, FinOps empowers organizations to unlock the full potential of their cloud investments.

Through a combination of strategic alignment, operational efficiency, and cultural transformation, FinOps enables organizations to optimize their cloud usage and costs effectively.

In the next chapter, we will learn Core FinOps Principles and Framework.

Key Terms

- **FinOps (Financial Operations)**: A cultural practice promoting collaboration between finance, IT, and business teams to manage cloud spending effectively, ensuring accountability, transparency, and optimization
- **Visibility**: The practice of tracking cloud costs in real-time using tools like tagging, dashboards, and reporting to eliminate wasteful spending
- **Accountability**: Assigning ownership of cloud costs to teams driving consumption, fostering responsible decision-making
- **Optimization**: Continuous improvement of cloud efficiency through rightsizing, automation, and lifecycle management

- **Tagging:** Labeling cloud resources (for example, by department or project) to categorize costs and allocate budgets accurately
- **Rightsizing:** Adjusting cloud resource allocations (for example, compute instances) to match actual usage, avoiding overprovisioning
- **Zombie Assets:** Idle or underutilized cloud resources (for example, unused servers, stale data) that incur unnecessary costs
- **Lifecycle Management:** Regularly auditing and decommissioning unused resources to reduce waste
- **Reserved Instances:** Prepaid cloud capacity agreements offering discounts in exchange for long-term commitments
- **Cost per Customer:** A metric linking cloud expenses to individual subscribers, enabling strategic alignment with growth

Questions

1. Explain how FinOps fosters collaboration between finance and engineering teams.
2. What are the three pillars of FinOps, and how do they contribute to cost management?
3. How did tagging resources help the global e-commerce company during Black Friday?
4. Why is lifecycle management critical in cloud cost optimization?
5. Discuss the role of FinOps in achieving sustainability goals, using Etsy as an example.

Multiple Choice Questions

1. What does FinOps emphasize?
    a. Cutting costs at all expenses
    b. Aligning cloud spending with business value
    c. Centralizing IT control
    d. Eliminating cloud adoption

2. What is a "zombie asset"?
    a. A hacked server
    b. An idle resource incurring costs
    c. A reserved instance
    d. A tagged database
3. Which tool provides real-time cloud cost visibility?
    a. AWS Cost Explorer
    b. Microsoft Excel
    c. Google Analytics
    d. Salesforce CRM
4. Which FinOps pillar involves assigning cost ownership?
    a. Inform
    b. Optimise
    c. Operate
    d. Automation

Answers

1. b
2. b
3. a
4. a

CHAPTER 2

Core FinOps Principles and Framework

Introduction

Managing cloud costs is not a one-time task, but an ongoing process. That is where the FinOps framework comes in. Think of it as a roadmap for taking control of your cloud spending. It is not just about cutting costs; it is about making smarter decisions, fostering cross-functional collaboration, and driving measurable business value.

Imagine navigating a bustling city without a map. You might stumble upon shortcuts or scenic routes by accident, but you would likely waste time and resources along the way. Similarly, without a structured approach to cloud financial management, organizations risk overspending, inefficiencies, and missed opportunities for innovation.

The FinOps framework provides that much required map–a clear and actionable methodology for aligning cloud investments with business goals. It combines the disciplines of finance, operations, and engineering to ensure organizations can maximize the value of their cloud investments while maintaining cost discipline.

At the heart of the FinOps framework lies the FinOps lifecycle, which is a continuous, iterative process that helps teams manage cloud financial operations in a dynamic environment. The lifecycle consists of three core phases that indicate how money is being spent in different areas. By embedding the FinOps framework into your cloud strategy, you not only gain better control over your costs, you also build a culture of accountability, transparency, and continuous improvement.

By the end of this chapter, you will have a comprehensive understanding of how the FinOps lifecycle can transform your organization's approach to cloud financial management. Whether you are a startup or a Fortune 500 company, these principles will help you unlock the full potential of your cloud investments.

Structure

In this chapter, we will cover the following topics:

- FinOps Principles and Guiding Concepts
- FinOps Domain and Capabilities
- Overview of the FinOps lifecycle (Inform, Optimize, Operate)
- Goals and Outcomes of Each Phase

FinOps Principles and Guiding Concepts

Cloud environments are dynamic, they grow, shrink, and evolve based on business demands. Without a systematic approach to managing these changes, costs can spiral out of control. The FinOps lifecycle addresses this challenge by providing a structured yet flexible framework that adapts to your organization's unique needs.

Consider a global e-commerce company preparing for Black Friday sales. During peak traffic periods, they need to scale resources quickly to ensure seamless customer experiences. But once the rush is over, they must scale back to avoid unnecessary expenses.

The FinOps lifecycle helps them navigate this complexity by providing visibility into costs, optimizing resource usage, and embedding cost-aware practices into daily workflows. By embracing the FinOps lifecycle, organizations can turn cloud spending from a liability into a strategic asset. It is not just about saving money, but about creating a culture of accountability, transparency, and continuous improvement.

A Sneak Peek at the Phases

Before diving into the details, let us briefly introduce the three phases of the FinOps lifecycle:

- **Inform**: The first phase focuses on creating visibility of your cloud costs. You cannot optimize what you cannot measure, so this phase lays the foundation for everything else.
- **Optimize**: Once you know where your money is going, the next step is to make sure you are spending it wisely. This phase is all about finding inefficiencies and eliminating waste.
- **Operate**: The final phase embeds FinOps principles into your organization's DNA. It ensures that cloud cost management becomes a sustainable, ongoing practice rather than a one-off initiative.

Each phase is interconnected, forming a continuous cycle that keeps organizations agile and adaptable in the face of evolving business needs.

Real-World Impact

To illustrate the power of the FinOps lifecycle, consider the example of Airbnb. The company faced significant challenges managing its AWS costs as it scaled globally. By implementing the FinOps lifecycle, Airbnb achieved a 35% reduction in computing costs while maintaining exceptional service quality.

The company achieved this feat by gaining visibility into its spending (Inform), identified inefficiencies and optimized resources (Optimize). It also embedded cost-aware practices into their engineering culture (Operate). The immediately visible result was a scalable and efficient cloud strategy that supported their rapid growth.

FinOps Domains and Capabilities

Think of FinOps as building four core competencies that help your organization master its technology spending. These aren't steps you complete one after another; they are ongoing capabilities you develop together, like learning to juggle multiple balls at once. And it is not just about the cloud anymore–FinOps teams today are tackling everything from data centers to SaaS subscriptions to AI tools.

The Four Core Domains

The practice of FinOps is structured around four interconnected domains that together form a comprehensive operating model for cloud financial management. These domains–Understanding Cloud Usage and Cost, Performance Management and Benchmarking, Real-Time Decision Making, and Cloud Rate Optimization–work in concert to create a holistic approach that balances cost efficiency with operational performance and business value.

Understanding Cloud Use and Cost

This domain establishes the foundation for FinOps by gathering comprehensive data about technology usage and costs. Think of it as becoming a detective for your tech spending–you need to know where every dollar is going before you can make smart decisions about expenditures.

[This aligns with Exam Objective 2: Data Analysis and Showback, which focuses on establishing visibility, implementing proper cost allocation methodologies, and creating meaningful reports that enable data-driven decision making across the organization.]

Organizations develop capabilities to:

- **Collect direct and imputed cloud and technology costs and usage data**: For example, tracking not just your AWS bill, but also understanding the hidden costs like data transfer charges, or the true cost of that "free tier" service that's now generating significant egress fees.

- **Implement observability, utilization, and sustainability monitoring:** Like setting up dashboards that show your database is only using 20% of its capacity during off-peak hours, or monitoring carbon footprint alongside cost metrics.
- **Define organizational metadata for categorization and allocation:** Creating a consistent tagging strategy where every resource shows which team owns it, which project it supports, and which cost center should be charged (instead of having everything labeled "`production-server-1`").
- **Establish reporting and analytics processes:** Building automated reports that show engineering teams their monthly spend trends, or creating executive dashboards that translate technical metrics into business impact.
- **Create data frameworks that support all other FinOps domains:** Setting up the data infrastructure that lets you answer questions like "What did our mobile app cost us to run last quarter?" or "How much did we spend on AI/ML workloads this year?"

Quantifying Business Value

This domain connects technology spend with business outcomes, helping everyone understand what they're getting for their money. You become the translator between finance and engineering, showing how every infrastructure dollar drives real business results.

[This corresponds to Exam Objective 1: FinOps Principles and Framework and Exam Objective 3: Rate Optimization, emphasizing the need to connect technical metrics with business outcomes, demonstrate ROI, and ensure that optimization efforts deliver measurable value rather than just cost reduction.]

Key Capabilities

- Map monetary and non-monetary costs to business value and budgets - For instance, showing that the $50,000 monthly spend on your recommendation engine directly drives $500,000 in additional revenue, or demonstrating how investing in faster deployment tools reduces time-to-market by two weeks
- Develop forecasting using historical data and future business plans - Using last year's Black Friday traffic patterns to predict this year's infrastructure needs, or modeling how launching in three new markets will impact your database costs

- Establish and measure technical and organizational KPIs - Tracking metrics like "cost per customer acquisition" or "infrastructure cost as percentage of revenue," rather than just looking at absolute spend numbers
- Perform benchmarking across teams, business units, and with external organizations - Comparing your e-commerce team's cost-per-transaction against industry standards, or seeing how your mobile team's efficiency compares to your web team's
- Demonstrate ROI and value creation from technology investments - Proving that the migration to containers saved 30% on compute costs while improving deployment speed, or showing how the new monitoring tools prevented three outages that would have cost $100K each

Optimizing Cloud Use and Cost

This domain focuses on ensuring resources provide value and are purchased at optimal rates. It is where you roll up your sleeves and start making your infrastructure both more efficient and more cost-effective, without breaking anything important.

[This directly supports Exam Objective 4: Usage Optimization and Exam Objective 5: FinOps Tools and Services, which cover the practical implementation of optimization strategies, automation tools, and the technical capabilities needed to right-size resources and eliminate waste at scale.]

Organizations Build Capabilities to:

- **Rightsize resources and eliminate waste**: Discovering that your development environment is running on the same massive instances as production (costing $5,000/month when $500 would do), or finding orphaned resources from that project that got cancelled six months ago
- **Manage resource types, timing, and consumption amounts**: Switching batch processing jobs to spot instances for 70% savings, or automatically scaling down staging environments overnight and on weekends
- **Optimize rates through reserved instances, committed use discounts, and negotiations**: Committing to a 3-year reserved instance plan that cuts your compute costs by 40%, or negotiating enterprise discounts with your SaaS vendors based on actual usage patterns
- **Implement architecture modernization and sustainability considerations**: Refactoring a monolithic application to microservices that can scale independently (reducing waste), or choosing ARM-based instances that cost 20% less and have lower carbon footprint
- **Manage licensed and consumption-based SaaS products efficiently**: Right-sizing your Slack or Zoom licenses based on actual active users, or optimizing your Snowflake usage by implementing better data retention policies

- **Automate optimization processes and orchestration:** Setting up auto-scaling that responds to real traffic patterns, or automated scripts that shut down development resources during nights and weekends (saving $10,000/month with zero impact)

Managing the FinOps Practice

This domain enables continuous improvement and organizational alignment. The technical optimization is only half the battle - you need everyone working together and making cost-conscious decisions every day.

[This aligns with Exam Objective 6: People and Culture, which emphasizes cross-functional collaboration, role clarity, and building a culture of shared accountability—key components of a mature FinOps practice where everyone takes ownership of technology spending decisions.]

It Encompasses Capabilities for:

- **Effective FinOps operation and governance**: Establishing monthly cost reviews where each team explains their spending trends, or creating approval workflows for resources over certain thresholds (like requiring manager approval for instances larger than the normal)
- **Organization-wide enablement and education**: Running "FinOps 101" workshops for new engineers, or creating self-service cost dashboards that let developers see the impact of their deployment decisions in real-time
- **Cross-functional collaboration with all business personas**: Facilitating monthly meetings where finance, engineering, and product teams align on spending priorities, or creating shared KPIs that everyone can understand and optimize
- **Process standardization and maturity development**: Implementing standard tagging policies across all teams, or establishing incident response procedures for when spending spikes unexpectedly (like that time someone accidentally launched 1,000 instances)
- **Cultural transformation to embed FinOps principles**: Making cost consideration part of architecture reviews, or celebrating teams that achieve significant optimizations (like the team that reduced their monthly bill by $25,000 through smart caching)
- **Continuous improvement of the FinOps practice itself**: Regularly reviewing and updating your FinOps processes, gathering feedback from teams on what's working and what is not, or expanding your practice to cover new technology areas like AI/ML or edge computing

Implementation Guidelines

- **Work on Everything at Once**: Do not try to perfect one area before moving to the next. You will be most successful when you're making progress on all four areas simultaneously, even if it feels chaotic at first.
- **Customize for Your Reality**: Not every company needs every capability. A startup's FinOps practice will look very different from that of a Fortune 500 company. Focus on building the capabilities that will actually move the needle for your organization.
- **Everyone Needs the Basics**: While the specific capabilities vary, every company using cloud technology will end up doing some work in all four areas. You cannot skip any of them entirely.
- **It is All Connected**: These four areas feed into each other constantly. Your cost visibility informs your optimization decisions, which impact your business value calculations, which require organizational change management. Trying to do just one in isolation will not work.

When you successfully build capabilities across all four areas, you will have created something valuable: a FinOps culture where technology spending decisions are transparent, intentional, and aligned with what your business actually needs to succeed. This comprehensive approach ensures that you are not just optimizing costs, but building sustainable practices that scale with your organization and deliver long-term business value.

Overview of the FinOps lifecycle

To successfully manage cloud financials, organizations follow a structured approach known as the FinOps lifecycle. This lifecycle is made up of three key phases–Inform, Optimize, and Operate–that guide teams from gaining visibility to driving efficiency and embedding cost accountability into daily operations.

Phase 1: Inform – Shining a Light on Cloud Costs

Imagine trying to manage your household budget without knowing where your money is going. You would probably overspend on things you do not need and miss opportunities to save. The same principle applies to cloud spending. If you cannot see where your money is going, you cannot make smart decisions about it.

The Inform phase is all about creating visibility of your cloud costs. It is the foundation of FinOps because you cannot optimize what you cannot measure. Without visibility, cloud spending becomes a black box, and teams provision resources without understanding their financial impact, leading to wasted budgets and unused assets.

Think of it this way, in traditional IT environments, costs are predictable and fixed. But the cloud operates differently; it is dynamic, scalable, and variable. This flexibility is one of its greatest strengths, but it also introduces several complexities. Without proper oversight, organizations risk losing control of their spending.

A core tenet of the FinOps Foundation framework is that data must be transformed into an "actionable and timely narrative," moving beyond raw numbers to provide a clear story that drives business decisions. This is the fundamental purpose of the Inform phase. Let us explore how this phase works, along with key activities and real-world examples highlighting its importance.

Key Activities

- **Tagging Resources:** Tagging is like labeling your cloud resources so that you know who is using which resource and why. For example, you might tag resources by team (for example, "Marketing"), environment (for example, "Production"), or project (for example, "New Website Launch"). This matters because when everyone knows what they are responsible for, it is easier to hold teams accountable for their spending. Tagging transforms raw data into actionable insights, enabling better decision-making.

  Real-World Example: A retail company started tagging all its cloud resources by department. Within months, they discovered that one team was running unused servers, costing them $30,000 a month. Once they shut those down, they saved big.

  Expert Insight: "Tagging is the cornerstone of cloud cost management," says Sarah Johnson, a senior FinOps consultant at Bairny&Co. "It is not just about categorizing resources–it is about creating accountability and transparency."

  How to Get Started:

  1. Start small by tagging critical resources such as databases, storage buckets, and compute instances
  2. Use automated tools to enforce tagging policies and prevent untagged resources from being deployed
  3. Regularly review tags to ensure they remain accurate and relevant

- **Generating Cost Reports**: Tools such as AWS Cost Explorer, Azure Cost Management, and third-party platforms such as CloudHealth make it easy to track spending. These tools provide detailed breakdowns of where your money is going, helping you identify inefficiencies and opportunities for savings.

Real-World Example: A SaaS provider used AWS Cost Explorer to identify unused EC2 instances. They shut them down and immediately saved $50,000 a month. Not bad for a few clicks, right?

Best Practices:

- Schedule regular reports to monitor trends and anomalies
- Break down costs by department, project, or environment to pinpoint areas of concern
- Share insights with stakeholders to foster collaboration and accountability

Challenges: While generating reports is straightforward, interpreting the data can be tricky. For instance, a sudden spike in costs might indicate a legitimate business need, or it could signal waste. That is why context is the key.

- **Real-Time Monitoring:** Imagine getting an alert when your cloud bill spikes unexpectedly. That is what real-time monitoring does. It helps you catch issues before they spiral out of control.

Real-World Example: A retail company set up alerts during the holiday season to monitor spikes in traffic. When they saw costs rising faster than expected, they adjusted their infrastructure to avoid overspending.

Benefits of Real-Time Monitoring:

- Prevents runaway costs by identifying anomalies early
- Enables proactive adjustments, such as scaling resources up or down based on demand
- Builds trust between finance and engineering teams by providing transparency into spending patterns

How to Implement:

- Use cloud-native tools such as AWS CloudWatch or Azure Monitor to set up alerts
- Define thresholds for cost spikes and resource usage to trigger notifications
- Combine monitoring with automation to address issues automatically (for example, shutting down idle instances)

Challenges: While the benefits of visibility are clear, implementing these practices is not always easy. Here are some common challenges:

- **Adopting Tagging Policies:** Getting teams to adopt tagging policies can be tough at first. Some people see it as extra work, but it pays off eventually.

Solution:

- Educate teams on the importance of tagging and how it supports organizational goals
- Make tagging mandatory through governance policies and automated enforcement

- **Incomplete Data**: Without consistent tagging, your data might be incomplete, which makes it harder to spot inefficiencies.

  Solution:

  - Conduct audits to identify untagged or mislabeled resource
  - Use machine learning tools to analyze usage patterns and fill in gaps

- **Resistance to Change**

  Teams may resist new processes, especially if they disrupt existing workflows. Solution:

  - Involve teams in the design and implementation of tagging and reporting systems
  - Highlight success stories to demonstrate the value of visibility

Phase Recap: Inform – Shining a Light on Cloud Costs

- Established visibility as the foundation for FinOps by introducing tagging, cost reporting, and real-time monitoring. This ensures teams understand not just how much they spend—but *why* they are spending it.
- Implemented tagging strategies to create accountability and enable cost attribution by team, project, and environment.
- Leveraged cost reporting tools and alerts to identify inefficiencies, prevent cost overruns, and foster collaboration between finance and engineering.

Real-World FinOps in Action: Spotify

The theoretical principles of FinOps are best understood through the concrete successes of organizations that have embedded them into their culture. Spotify's journey provides a powerful, real-world blueprint for scaling cloud financial management within a dynamic, engineering-driven environment.

Challenge: Spotify.[1] was experiencing a rapid surge in cloud costs but lacked clear visibility into which teams, regions, or workloads were driving up the expenditure.

Solution: They implemented a robust tagging strategy by labeling cloud resources by team, region, and workload to gain granular visibility into usage and spending patterns.

Outcome:

- 20% reduction in overall cloud costs
- Strengthened accountability across engineering teams
- Improved cross-functional collaboration between finance, engineering, and operations

Lessons Learned:

- Start with tagging to drive visibility and ownership
- Automate tagging policies to reduce manual work and improve consistency
- Foster collaboration by making cost data accessible and actionable across teams

Turning Visibility into Action: The Inform phase is where FinOps begins. By shining a light on cloud costs, organizations can uncover inefficiencies, eliminate waste, and create a foundation for smarter decision-making.

As one industry leader put it:

> "Visibility is not just a tool; it is a mindset. When teams understand the financial impact of their actions, they make choices that drive value." – *Marcelo Escudero, Cloud Consultant at Anida Latam* anidalatam.com

By embracing the principles of the **Inform phase**, businesses can navigate the complexities of the digital age with confidence, achieving both financial and operational excellence. With FinOps, the sky is the limit–literally.

Phase 2: Optimize – Making Every Dollar Count

Once you know where your money is going, the next step is to make sure you are spending it wisely. That is where the optimizing phase comes in. This phase is all about finding inefficiencies and eliminating waste. Think of it as spring cleaning for your cloud environment; you declutter what you do not need, organize what you do, and ensure everything serves a purpose.

---

[1] Spotify's tagging strategy and FinOps-driven cloud cost reduction efforts were highlighted in "Zoom, Spotify, and others slashed their cloud costs by millions – how did they do it?", CAST AI, dev.to,

Optimization goes beyond cutting costs and is about making every dollar count. By aligning your cloud resources with actual needs, you can reduce waste without compromising performance or user experience. For example, when you are running a small database on a massive server, not only are you wasting money, but you are also underutilizing valuable resources that could be redirected elsewhere.

As one FinOps practitioner put it:

> "Optimization is like fine-tuning an engine. You are not stripping it down; you are making it run smoother and more efficiently." – *John Grubb, FinOps Expert and Founder of The FinOperator Source: https://www.thefinoperator.com/p/finops-is-performance-optimization*

By embracing the principles of the **Optimize phase**, businesses can navigate the complexities of the digital age with confidence, achieving both financial and operational excellence.

FinOps unlocks limitless possibilities for innovation and efficiency.

Let us dive deeper into the key activities that define this phase, along with real-world examples that highlight their impact:

Key Activities:

- **Rightsizing** means matching your cloud resources to your actual needs. For instance, if a database cluster is overprovisioned, you can downsize it to save costs without impacting performance.

  Real-World Example: A financial services firm resized its database instances and cut costs by 15%. It is like downsizing from a mansion to a cozy apartment. You still get what you need but at a fraction of the cost.

  Expert Insight:

  "Rightsizing is one of the easiest ways to achieve quick wins in cloud cost optimization. It's low-hanging fruit that delivers immediate ROI." – *John Renne, FinOps Practitioner and Co-host of FinOpsPod* Source: FinOpsPod 14: https://www.finops.org/community/finops-podcast

  How to Get Started:

  - Use tools such as AWS Trusted Advisor or Azure Advisor to identify overprovisioned resources
  - Analyze usage patterns to determine the right size for each resource
  - Test changes in non-production environments before rolling them out widely

- **Reserved Instances and Savings Plans**

  If you know you will need certain resources for the long haul, you can lock in discounts by purchasing reserved instances or savings plans. These options offer significant savings compared to on-demand pricing.

  Real-World Example: A healthcare organization saved 40% on costs by committing to reserved instances. It is like buying a subscription instead of paying full price every time, as it is more predictable and cost-effective.

  Challenges: Forecasting future usage for reserved instances requires some guesswork, which can be intimidating for teams unfamiliar with usage patterns. However, tools such as predictive analytics can help mitigate this risk.

  Best Practices:

  - Start small by committing to reserved instances for predictable workloads (for example databases or long-running applications)
  - Use savings plans for flexible commitments that apply across multiple services
  - Regularly review usage to ensure reserved instances are being fully utilized

- **Auto-Scaling and Spot Instances:** Auto-scaling adjusts your resources based on demand, so you only pay for what you use. Spot instances take this a step further–they let you use spare capacity at a fraction of the cost.

  Real-World Example: An e-commerce platform used spot instances for batch processing and reduced costs by 60%. It is like catching a flight on standby; you get a great deal if you are flexible enough.

  Best Practices: To maximize the benefits of auto-scaling and spot instances, organizations should implement robust monitoring and alert systems. This ensures that critical workloads are not interrupted during peak demand periods.

  Additional Insights:

  - Use auto-scaling policies to handle traffic spikes during events such as Black Friday or holiday sales
  - Combine spot instances with on-demand instances to balance cost savings and reliability
  - Leverage tools such as Kubernetes or AWS Lambda for dynamic scaling and workload management

- **Lifecycle Management**

  Lifecycle management ensures that unused or underutilized resources are decommissioned promptly. This includes deleting old snapshots, terminating idle instances, and archiving stale data.

  Real-World Example: Dropbox identified 200TB of stale data sitting unused in S3 buckets. By deleting these files, they saved millions annually.

  Expert Tip: "Lifecycle management is often overlooked, but it is one of the most impactful practices," says Mark Thompson, a cloud economist. "Automating cleanup processes can yield significant savings with minimal effort."

  How to Implement:

  - Set up automated scripts to delete unused resources after a set period
  - Use lifecycle policies in AWS S3 or Azure Blob Storage to transition data to cheaper storage tiers
  - Conduct regular audits to identify and eliminate zombie assets

Challenges

While optimization offers significant benefits, it is not without its challenges:

- **Balancing cost savings with performance:** Cutting corners can hurt user experience, so it is crucial to strike the right balance
- **Forecasting future usage:** Committing to reserved instances requires some guesswork, which can be intimidating for teams unfamiliar with usage patterns
- **Resistance to change:** Teams may resist changes that impact their workflows, even if they lead to cost savings

Phase Recap: Optimize – Making Every Dollar Count

- **Rightsize cloud resources** to match actual usage, achieving quick wins and improving resource efficiency, which is just like downsizing a mansion to a cozy apartment without losing comfort
- **Leverage Reserved Instances and Savings Plans** to lock in long-term discounts, balancing flexibility and predictability in cloud spend
- **Implement auto-scaling and spot instances** to respond dynamically to demand, reducing costs by up to 60% while maintaining performance
- **Enforce lifecycle management** to eliminate unused or underutilized assets, uncovering hidden savings like Dropbox's millions saved on stale S3 data

Real-World FinOps in Action: Airbnb

Challenge: Airbnb needed to manage massive traffic spikes without letting cloud costs spiral out of control. The company's rapid global growth meant unpredictable usage patterns across multiple services, including search, booking, and payments. Engineering teams required both **high availability and low latency** during peak periods, while finance teams needed **visibility into cost drivers** to prevent budget overruns. Balancing performance, user experience, and cost efficiency became a critical operational priority.

Solution: They used a combination of rightsizing, reserved instances, and auto-scaling to optimize compute usage dynamically.

Outcome:

- Reduced compute costs by **35%**
- Scaled infrastructure seamlessly during seasonal peaks
- Established cost-efficiency without sacrificing performance

Key Takeaways:

- Start small measurable wins build trust and momentum
- Automate repetitive cost tasks like monitoring and cleanup
- Leverage scaling tools to align infrastructure with demand

Phase 3: Operate – Embedding FinOps into Daily Workflows

The Operate phase is where FinOps becomes part of an organization's DNA. It is not enough to merely inform and optimize; you need to embed these practices into your daily workflows. This phase is all about creating a sustainable FinOps culture that supports long-term success.

Think of it this way: FinOps is not a one-time project, but a mindset. When teams embrace FinOps as part of their everyday responsibilities, they start making smarter decisions by default. This cultural shift ensures that cloud cost management becomes a natural extension of how people work rather than an afterthought or a burden.

Let us explore the key activities that define this phase, along with real-world examples and strategies for embedding FinOps into your organization's fabric:

Key Activities:

- **Governance Policies:** Governance is about setting rules for how resources are provisioned and managed. For example, you might require mandatory tagging, enforce spending limits, or restrict who can spin up new instances. These policies create guardrails that prevent overspending while empowering teams to innovate responsibly.

Real-World Example: A tech startup enforced mandatory tagging for all new resources. Suddenly, teams had a clearer picture of their spending, and accountability skyrocketed.

Expert Insight: "FinOps is the practice of bringing financial accountability to the variable spend model of cloud, enabling distributed teams to make business trade-offs between speed, cost, and quality," says **J.R. Storment, Co-founder of the FinOps Foundation**. goodreads.com.

Best Practices:

- Require tagging for all cloud resources (for example, by team, project, or environment)
- Implement approval workflows for high-cost actions, such as provisioning large instances
- Use tools such as AWS Service Control Policies (SCPs) or Azure Policy to enforce compliance automatically

- **Automation:** Automation takes repetitive tasks off your plate so you can focus on the big picture. For example, you can set up scripts to shut down idle instances overnight, delete unused storage, or scale resources dynamically based on demand.

  Real-World Example: Bairny&Co automated the shutdown of unused development environments and saved $20,000 a month. It is like having a robot turn off the lights when no one is home.

  Challenges: While automation saves time and money, implementing it requires copious efforts. Teams may resist changes if they feel their workflows are being disrupted.

  How to Get Started:

  - Identify repetitive tasks that can be automated, such as cost monitoring or cleanup processes
  - Use infrastructure-as-code (IaC) tools such as Terraform or AWS CloudFormation to standardize resource provisioning
  - Leverage serverless functions (for example, AWS Lambda) for lightweight automation tasks

- **Budget Management:** Setting budgets and tracking spending are crucial for staying on track. Monthly reviews help you catch overspending early and adjust course before costs spiral out of control.

Real-World Example: A logistics company implemented monthly budget reviews and avoided surprise bills. It is like checking your bank account regularly to make sure that nothing is overdrawn.

Expert Insight: "Budgets are more than numbers; they are communication tools," says Jesse Hanks, Senior FinOps Practitioner at Bairny & Co. "They align teams around shared goals and foster collaboration.".

How to Implement:

- o Set clear budgets for departments, projects, or teams based on historical data and forecasts
- o Use alerts and dashboards to monitor spending in real-time
- o Conduct regular reviews to identify trends, anomalies, and areas for improvement

- **Cultural Shift:** Encouraging teams to take ownership of their cloud spending is the most critical aspect of the Operate phase. When people feel responsible, they are more likely to make smarter decisions.

  Celebrate Wins–Big and Small: Whether it is saving $5,000 or $50,000, every dollar counts. Recognizing achievements reinforces positive behaviors and motivates teams to continue improving.

  Example: A SaaS provider celebrated a team that reduced their database costs by 15% through rightsizing. The recognition not only boosted the overall morale but also inspired other teams to follow suit.

  Strategies for Building a Strong FinOps Culture:

  - o Foster open communication between finance, engineering, and leadership teams
  - o Encourage experimentation and reward innovative solutions to cost challenges
  - o Provide training and resources to help teams understand the financial impact of their decisions

Operate Phase Recap

- **FinOps becomes a mindset.** It is not a one-time initiative but is reflected in how teams work every day.
- **Governance and automation drive consistency.** Enforced tagging, policies, and scripted actions reduce waste and risks
- **Culture enables sustainability.** Empowered teams make smarter decisions and stay aligned with business goals

- **Recognition fuels momentum.** Celebrating cost-saving wins builds a cost-conscious, collaborative culture

Real-World FinOps in Action: Capital One

Challenge: Capital One[2] , a leading US bank and financial services company, aimed to reduce ballooning cloud costs while improving developer efficiency and enforcing strong governance. As a highly regulated enterprise with a broad range of digital services–from mobile banking apps to AI-driven fraud detection–Capital One needed to balance financial accountability with rapid innovation and secure, compliant operations.

Solution:

- Embedded FinOps into engineering workflows by aligning teams across finance, operations, and development
- Built internal tools to track spending, enforce tagging policies, and automatically shut down unused resources
- Prioritized cultural change, making cost accountability part of engineering KPIs

Outcome:

- Achieved a **25% reduction in cloud costs**
- Created a culture of shared financial responsibility and data-driven optimization

Lessons Learned:

- Start small by integrating FinOps into daily engineering habits
- Use automation to eliminate waste and free up strategic focus
- Reinforce behavioral change by celebrating cost-saving wins

The Continuous Cycle of FinOps

FinOps is not a one-and-done deal. After you have informed, optimized, and operated, you go back to the beginning and start again as cloud environments are always changing along with business needs. The FinOps lifecycle is a continuous cycle that keeps you agile and adaptable.

---

[2] "*How Capital One Controls Cloud Costs,*" BizTech Magazine.

https://www.biztechmagazine.com/article/2025/08/how-capital-one-controls-cloud-costs

Why It Works

This iterative process delivers sustained value because it is grounded in core operational principles that transform cloud financial management from a static cost-control exercise into a dynamic, business-enabling capability.

- **Adaptability:** When priorities shift, you can adjust quickly. For example, during peak sales periods, you might temporarily increase capacity and then scale back afterwards.
- **Scalability:** As your business grows, FinOps scales with you. Whether you are launching new products or entering new markets, FinOps ensures that cloud spending aligns with your evolving needs.
- **Sustainability:** Continuous improvement ensures long-term success. By regularly reviewing and refining your practices, you can stay ahead of inefficiencies and emerging challenges.

The Ripple Effect of a Strong FinOps Culture

When organizations embed FinOps into their daily workflows, the benefits extend far beyond cost savings:

- **Improved Collaboration:** Breaking down silos between finance, engineering, and leadership fosters trust and alignment. Teams work together to balance innovation with fiscal discipline.
- **Faster Decision-Making:** Real-time visibility enables quicker responses to changing market conditions. For example, an e-commerce company can scale resources dynamically during Black Friday sales without overspending.

Visual Representation:

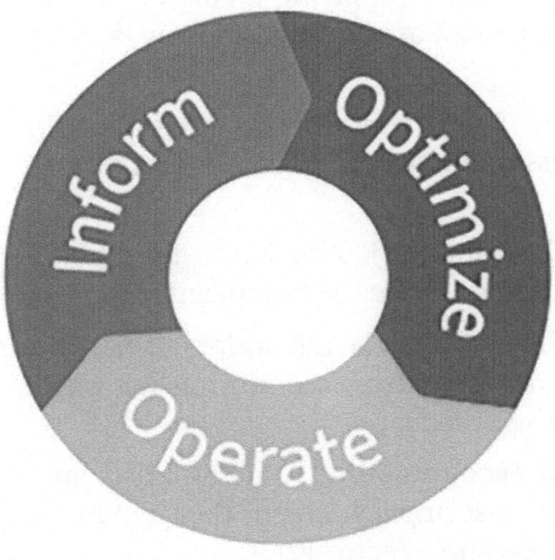

Figure 2.1: *FinOps Phases by FinOps Foundation*

Conclusion

FinOps is about creating a mindset where every decision adds value.

The Operate phase is where FinOps truly comes alive. By embedding governance policies, leveraging automation, managing budgets, and fostering a strong FinOps culture, organizations can ensure that cloud cost management becomes a sustainable, ongoing practice.

As one industry leader put it: "FinOps is not just about managing costs–it is about creating a mindset where every decision adds value. When you get it right, the possibilities are endless."

By embracing these principles, businesses can navigate the complexities of the digital age with confidence, achieving both financial and operational excellence.

With FinOps, the sky is the limit–literally.

The next chapter will explore on the Inform Phase.

Key Terms

- **FinOps**: A collaborative, cross-functional financial operating model for the cloud that brings together finance, technology, and business teams to drive value and accountability.
- **FinOps Lifecycle:** The continuous, iterative process of cloud financial management, consisting of three core phases: Inform (visibility), Optimize (action), and Operate (sustained practice).
- **Tagging:** The practice of applying metadata labels (tags) to cloud resources to enable accurate cost attribution, tracking, and accountability across teams and projects.
- **Cost Allocation:** The process of assigning and distributing cloud costs to specific business units, teams, or cost centers based on their actual resource consumption.
- **Governance**: The framework of policies, guardrails, and controls implemented to ensure cloud usage is secure, compliant, and cost-effective.
- **Automation:** The use of tools and scripts to perform repetitive tasks without manual intervention, such as monitoring for waste, enforcing policies, and cleaning up unused resources.
- **Cloud Financial Accountability:** A cultural principle that ensures every team understands the cost implications of their cloud usage and is empowered to manage their spending effectively.

Points to Remember

- FinOps is not just about cutting costs, but about maximizing value.
- The FinOps lifecycle is a continuous process of visibility, optimization, and sustainability.
- Collaboration between finance, engineering, and business teams is essential for creating a unified strategy where financial accountability, technical execution, and product goals are seamlessly aligned, transforming cloud financial management from a point of conflict into a source of competitive advantage.
- Tagging and cost visibility are foundational to understanding cloud spending
- Rightsizing, reserved instances, and auto-scaling are key optimization strategies.
- Governance, automation, and budget management are crucial for embedding FinOps into workflows.
- A strong FinOps culture encourages ownership, accountability, and continuous improvement.

Questions

1. Why is the FinOps lifecycle described as a continuous and iterative process?
2. How does tagging help in creating financial accountability in cloud environments?
3. What are the key differences between the Inform, Optimize, and Operate phases?
4. How can automation support the FinOps lifecycle?
5. What role does organizational culture play in the success of FinOps?
6. Discuss how Spotify used FinOps to reduce cloud costs by 20%.
7. What challenges might a company face when implementing FinOps, and how can they be overcome?
8. How does FinOps help align cloud spending with business goals?

Multiple Choice Questions

1. What is the primary goal of the Inform phase in the FinOps lifecycle?
   a. Reduce cloud costs
   b. Improve resource efficiency
   c. Provide visibility into cloud spending
   d. Automate cloud governance
2. Which of the following is NOT a core principle of FinOps?
   a. Collaboration
   b. Accountability
   c. Cost-Cutting Only
   d. Continuous Improvement
3. Which FinOps phase ensures that cost management becomes part of the organization's culture?
   a. Inform
   b. Optimize
   c. Operate
   d. Plan
4. What is the purpose of tagging cloud resources?
   a. To increase cloud performance
   b. To improve security
   c. To enable cost allocation and accountability
   d. To simplify deployment
5. Which of the following best describes the FinOps lifecycle?
   a. Linear and static
   b. One-time process
   c. Continuous and iterative
   d. Focused only on cost reduction

6. What does "rightsizing" refer to in the context of FinOps?
    a. Increasing team sizes
    b. Matching cloud resources to actual usage
    c. Reducing cloud vendors
    d. Hiring financial experts
7. Which company achieved a 35% reduction in computing costs by implementing FinOps practices?
    a. Spotify
    b. Capital One
    c. Airbnb
    d. Dropbox
8. Why is automation important in the Operate phase?
    a. It eliminates the need for cloud engineers.
    b. It reduces manual effort and scales FinOps practices.
    c. It increases cloud costs.
    d. It replaces governance policies.

Answers

1. c
2. c
3. c
4. c
5. c
6. b
7. c
8. b

CHAPTER 3

Inform Phase: Cloud Visibility and Allocation

Introduction

Imagine sitting down to manage your household budget, only to realize you have no idea where your money is going. You know that the bills are piling up but without a clear breakdown of expenses, making smart decisions is nearly impossible. Have you cut back on dining out? Cancelled unused memberships? Or maybe consolidated services for better rates? Even small inefficiencies can add up quickly without providing you visibility about things that matter, leaving you frustrated and financially strained.

Now, adopt this scenario to the world of cloud computing. Organizations face a similar challenge when managing their cloud costs. Bills are often full of cryptic line items such as "EC2 (Elastic Compute Cloud) Instances," "Data Transfer Out", or "S3 (Simple Storage Service) Buckets". Engineers spin up servers for testing, while developers provision resources for new features, and marketing teams deploy campaigns. However, they often do it all without fully understanding the financial impact of their actions. The result is often seen in wasted budgets, unused assets, and missed opportunities for savings.

This is where the Inform phase of FinOps comes in—it is where the journey begins. Think of it as turning on the lights in a dark room. Without any visibility into expenditures, cloud spending becomes a black box. Teams provision resources based on technical needs but lack insight into how those decisions affect the bottom line. This disconnect leads to inefficiencies, such as idle servers running unnecessarily, overprovisioned databases draining budgets, and redundant storage eating away at margins.

In today's dynamic cloud environments, costs can spiral out of control if left unchecked. Unlike traditional IT setups, where expenses are predictable and fixed, the cloud operates on a pay-as-you-go model. While this flexibility is one of its greatest strengths, it also introduces complexity. For example, scaling resources up during peak demand might seem like a great idea, until you forget to scale them back down afterward. Similarly, provisioning large instances "just to be safe" can lead to overspending without delivering proportional value.

We will also discuss tagging strategies, tools for cost visibility, and how to communicate insights to stakeholders. By the end of this chapter, the readers will have a roadmap for gaining control over your cloud finances and setting the stage for future optimization efforts.

Structure

In this chapter, we will cover the following topics:

- Gather cloud cost data to create a clear picture of spending patterns
- Allocate costs effectively to ensure fairness and accountability
- Create transparency through reporting that empowers teams to act

Unlocking the Power of Cloud Visibility

Achieving true control over cloud spending begins with a fundamental prerequisite: the ability to see and understand every cost in detail. This critical process of gaining granular insight into your cloud environment is the essential first step toward informed decision-making and financial accountability.

The Problem with Cloud Costs

Cloud computing has revolutionized the way organizations operate by offering unparalleled flexibility and scalability. With just a few clicks, teams can spin up servers, deploy applications, and scale resources to meet demand. This agility empowers businesses to innovate faster and respond to real-time market fluctuations. However, this flexibility comes with significant unpredictability. Without proper visibility into cloud spending, organizations risk losing control of their budgets, leading to inefficiencies that can undermine the very benefits they seek to achieve.

Let us break down why visibility is so critical by examining the common challenges organizations face when managing cloud costs. The Inform phase is not just about uncovering waste—it is about transforming chaos into clarity. When teams understand where their money is going, they can start making smarter decisions. "As Mike Fuller, a founding Finops engineer at Atlassian, has stated, the goal is to build 'a culture of cost accountability,' where engineering teams are empowered to make efficient trade-offs."

By embracing the principles of the Inform phase, businesses can take the first step towards unlocking the full potential of their cloud investments.

The Challenges of Unchecked Cloud Spending

- **Overspending: The Silent Budget Killer:** In traditional IT environments, costs were predictable and fixed. Hardware purchases, maintenance contracts, and software licenses were planned and accounted for upfront. But in the cloud, resources are dynamic and on-demand. While this flexibility is one of the cloud's greatest strengths, it also introduces complexity. Teams may provision resources for testing or development and forget to decommission them afterward. This can be seen in the following example:

    - A developer spins up a virtual machine to test a new feature but leaves it running after the task is complete.
    - As a result, storage buckets accumulate redundant backups or outdated files that no one bothers to clean up.

    These seemingly small oversights can add up quickly. According to industry reports, 30%-40% of cloud spend is wasted on unused or underutilized resources. Without visibility, these inefficiencies often go unnoticed and quietly drain budgets month after month.

- **Budget Overruns: A CFO's Nightmare:** Finance teams often struggle to reconcile actual cloud spending with forecasts. Unlike traditional IT expenses, which are predictable and static, cloud costs fluctuate based on usage. This variability makes it difficult to create accurate budgets. For instance:

    - A sudden spike in traffic might lead to unexpected scaling of compute resources, driving up costs.
    - Reserved instances purchased for long-term savings may go underutilized if usage patterns change.

    When finance teams receive bloated cloud bills at the end of the month, they are left scrambling to explain the discrepancies. This lack of alignment between technical decisions and financial planning creates friction between departments and erodes trust.

- **Accountability Gaps: Who Owns the Bill?**

    In many organizations, cloud spending is treated as a shared pool of resources with no clear ownership or accountability. Engineers provision resources without considering their financial impact, while finance teams lack the technical context to understand line items such as "EC2 Instances" or "Data

Transfer Out." This ambiguity leads to accountability gaps, where no one takes responsibility for specific costs.

- For example, a marketing team launches a campaign using cloud-based analytics tools. If they do not track the associated costs, the expenses can spiral out of control without anyone noticing.
- Similarly, a product team might overprovision resources for a new feature, assuming someone else will monitor the budget.

Without visibility, it is impossible to assign ownership and hold teams accountable.

Solving Cost Challenges through the Inform Phase

The Inform phase of FinOps addresses these challenges head-on by providing a clear, comprehensive view of cloud spending. It ensures that everyone, be it engineers or executives, understands where the money is going and why. Here is how having visibility into expenditures transforms cloud cost management:

- **Eliminating Overspending Through Transparency:** By shining a light on cloud costs, organizations can identify and eliminate waste. Tools such as tagging, dashboards, and real-time monitoring make it easy to track resource usage and spending patterns. For example:
  - Tagging resources by department, project, or environment helps teams see exactly what they are paying for
  - Real-time alerts notify teams when costs exceed predefined thresholds, enabling proactive adjustments

  Armed with this information, teams can take immediate action to shut down unused resources, right size overprovisioned instances, and delete redundant data
- **Aligning Budgets with Business Needs:** Visibility bridges the gap between finance and engineering teams, enabling better collaboration and alignment. When finance teams understand the technical drivers of cloud costs and engineers know about the financial implications of their decisions, it becomes easier to create realistic budgets and forecasts.
  - For instance, a retail company preparing for Black Friday sales can use historical data to predict traffic spikes and allocate resources accordingly
  - Regular reviews of spending trends help organizations stay on track and avoid surprises at the end of the month

- **Fostering Accountability Across Teams**

  Visibility ensures that every dollar spent is tied to a specific team, project, or initiative. By assigning ownership of cloud costs, organizations can foster a culture of accountability. For example:

  - A SaaS provider might tag resources by customer account, allowing them to calculate the cost per user and optimize accordingly.
  - A healthcare organization could enforce mandatory tagging policies, ensuring that every resource is labeled with its purpose and owner.

  When teams know they are responsible for their spending, they are more likely to make cost-conscious decisions.

A Real-World Example: Atlassian's Visibility Journey

As Atlassian's cloud usage grew, so did its AWS bill—faster than expected and without much insight into where the costs were coming from.

To take back control, the company implemented a detailed tagging strategy, labeling resources by team, project, and environment. This improved visibility helped teams:

- Spot underused compute and storage resources that were quietly driving up costs
- Share quick wins in planning sessions such as rightsizing or retiring unused services

By focusing on visibility and accountability, Atlassian reduced cloud waste and strengthened collaboration between engineering and finance. Their journey shows how better insight leads to smarter decisions and stronger outcomes.[1]

Turning Chaos into Clarity

Managing cloud costs can feel overwhelming. It is like trying to navigate a storm without a compass. Bills climb faster than expected, resources sprawl across teams, and no one is quite sure who is responsible for what. That is where visibility comes in—not just to track spending, but to make sense of it.

The **Inform Phase** of FinOps is all about turning that chaos into clarity. It helps organizations go beyond just numbers on a dashboard and uncover the reasons behind cloud spending. By identifying the root causes of waste—whether it's idle resources,

---

[1]Atlassian improved cost efficiency by using tagging, automation, and chargeback—cutting waste and boosting team accountability. Source: Redress Compliance – FinOps Strategies for Controlling Cloud Spend

unclear ownership, or lack of accountability–teams gain the insights they need to make smarter, more confident decisions.

Something powerful happens when teams truly understand the impact of their choices. As one FinOps practitioner put it: "As J.R. *Storment, co-founder of the FinOps Foundation, has stated: "FinOps is a cultural practice that shifts cloud financial management from a reactive to a proactive, data-driven discipline."*[2]

With this kind of shared understanding, engineering, finance, and leadership begin operating with a true strategic alignment. Cloud costs stop being a pain point and start becoming a strategic asset, which further fuels innovation instead of slowing it down. This is the real magic of FinOps, where people obtain the clarity they need to turn uncertainties into opportunities.

Gathering Cloud Cost Data: Unpacking the Essentials

Every action you take in the cloud leaves a financial footprint. Whether it is spinning up a virtual machine, storing data in a bucket, or running queries on a managed database, these activities generate cost data. To effectively manage your cloud spending, you need to gather this data from various sources and consolidate it into actionable insights. But where exactly does this data come from, and how can you collect it efficiently? Let's learn about it in the following section:

Sources of Cloud Cost Data

The first and most accessible source of cost data is the cloud provider's built-in set of tools. These platforms offer dashboards, reports, and APIs to help you understand where your money is going and why. Here are a few key examples of such tools:

- **Native Cloud Provider Tools:** The first place to look for cost data is within the tools provided by the cloud vendor. These platforms are designed to give you detailed visibility into your spending patterns. Some of these tools are as follows:
    - **AWS Cost Explorer:** Provides granular breakdowns of AWS usage, including compute instances, storage, and data transfer costs
    - **Azure Cost Management:** Offers dashboards, budgets, and forecasting tools to track Azure spending

[2] Quote adapted from J.R. *Storment, co-founder of the FinOps Foundation* insight shared in industry discussions and FinOps Foundation community events, emphasizing how cost transparency drives more thoughtful and accountable decision-making.

   - **Google Cloud Billing:** Aggregates cost data across Google Cloud services, with export options for deeper analysis

  These tools aggregate data from your cloud usage and present it through intuitive dashboards, reports, and APIs. They are especially useful for single-cloud environments and offer a clear view of where your money is going.

  Real-World Example: A retail company used AWS Cost Explorer to identify unused EC2 instances. By shutting them down, they saved $50,000 monthly, which was a significant win for their bottom line.

- **Third-Party Tools:** Achieving true cost clarity in a complex cloud environment requires a cohesive set of capabilities: comprehensive visibility, granular analytics, and automated governance. Third-party tools are often instrumental in bringing these components together.

  For organizations operating in multi-cloud environments, third-party platforms such as CloudHealth, Apptio, and Spot.io provide advanced analytics and automation capabilities. These tools integrate seamlessly with multiple cloud providers, offering a unified view of your spending.

   - **CloudHealth:** Helps optimize costs, improve governance, and enhance security across AWS, Azure, and Google Cloud
   - **Apptio:** Focuses on aligning IT spending with business outcomes and provides insights into cost drivers and ROI
   - **Spot.io:** This specializes in workload optimization, particularly for Kubernetes and containerized environments.

The Strategic Value of Third-Party Tools

These platforms often go beyond native tools, offering predictive analytics, anomaly detection, and automation features that streamline cost management.

Here is one such example in Action:

A SaaS provider using both AWS and Azure leveraged CloudHealth to consolidate their spending data. This enabled them to identify inefficiencies such as overprovisioned databases and idle resources, saving 20% annually.

- **Custom Scripts and Automation:** While third-party platforms offer broad capabilities, some scenarios demand a more specialized approach to cost management. Custom scripts and automation provide this targeted flexibility for unique organizational needs.

  For organizations with unique requirements, custom scripts can extract cost data directly from cloud provider APIs. This approach allows for tailored solutions that fit specific workflows.

- **API Integration:** Use APIs from AWS, Azure, or Google Cloud to pull raw cost data programmatically
- **Automation:** Automate data collection and reporting processes to reduce manual effort and errors

Here is a Use Case that illustrates how organizations can use custom scripts: A tech startup built a custom script to pull daily cost data from AWS and Azure APIs. They then visualized the data in an internal dashboard, enabling real-time monitoring and faster decision-making.

Challenges in Gathering Cloud Cost Data

While gathering cloud cost data is essential, it is not without its hurdles. Here are some common challenges that organizations face:

- **Data Fragmentation:** In multi-cloud environments, cost data is scattered across platforms, making it difficult to consolidate into a single source of truth. Without proper integration, teams may struggle to get a holistic view of their spending.

  Solution: Use third-party tools or build custom integrations to unify data from multiple cloud providers
- **Granularity Issues:** Some tools may lack the level of detail needed to pinpoint inefficiencies. For example, a report might show high storage costs but fail to specify which buckets or files are driving those expenses.

  Solution: Standardize tagging policies to categorize resources by team, project, or environment. This ensures you can drill down into specific areas of concern
- **Latency:** Cloud cost data is not always real-time. It can take hours or even days for the usage stats to reflect in billing reports. This delay can make it challenging for organizations to respond quickly and tackle unexpected spikes.

  Solution: Combine historical data with real-time monitoring tools to stay ahead of anomalies

Best Practices for Gathering Cloud Cost Data

To overcome these challenges and ensure accurate, actionable insights, follow these best practices:

- **Use APIs to Pull Raw Data:** Leverage APIs provided by cloud vendors to extract raw cost data. This gives you more control over how the data is processed and analyzed.

- **Standardize Naming Conventions and Tagging Policies:** Consistent tagging ensures that every resource is labeled appropriately, making it easier to track spending by department, project, or environment.

  Example: A global e-commerce company tagged resources by the campaign (for example, "Black Friday Promo") and monitored real-time usage to adjust capacity dynamically.

- **Automate Data Collection:** Manual processes are prone to errors and inefficiencies. Automating data collection reduces the risk of mistakes and frees up time for strategic initiatives. How to Start:
  - Use infrastructure-as-code (IaC) tools such as Terraform or AWS CloudFormation to standardize resource provisioning
  - Leverage serverless functions (for example, AWS Lambda) for lightweight automation tasks such as cost monitoring and cleanup
- **Leverage Dashboards and Alerts:** Visualizing data through dashboards helps teams spot trends and anomalies at a glance. Pair this with alerts to catch issues before they spiral out of control.

  Real-Time Monitoring Example: A retail company set up alerts during the holiday season to monitor spikes in traffic. When costs rose faster than expected, they adjusted their infrastructure to avoid overspending.

The Ripple Effect of Effective Data Gathering

When done right, gathering cloud cost data lays the foundation for smarter decision-making. It enables teams to:

- **Identify Waste:** Spot unused or underutilized resources and eliminate them promptly
- **Optimize Spending:** Right size instances, leverage reserved instances and use spot instances for cost-effective scaling
- **Foster Accountability:** Assign ownership of cloud costs to the teams driving consumption, encouraging mindful spending

Case Study: Dropbox: Dropbox identified 200TB of stale data sitting unused in S3 buckets. By deleting these files, they saved millions annually. This discovery was only possible because they had robust data-gathering practices in place.

Turning Data into Action

By leveraging native tools, third-party platforms, and custom solutions, organizations transform raw cloud cost data into a clear and actionable narrative of their spending.

By relying on native tools, third-party platforms, and custom solutions, organizations can gain a comprehensive view of their spending.

The FinOps Foundation Framework emphasizes that the ultimate goal is not just data collection, but empowering teams to: "Make informed, timely, and cost-effective decisions in the cloud."

By embracing best practices such as API integration, standardized tagging, and automation, businesses can turn raw data into actionable strategies.

Cost Allocation Methods and Tagging Strategies

Cost allocation is the systematic process of assigning cloud costs to specific teams, projects, or departments. It is not just about tracking expenses, but possessing a deep understanding about who is responsible for what, ensuring accountability across the organization. Without clear cost allocation, cloud spending can quickly become a tangled web of unattributed expenses, leaving finance teams frustrated and engineering teams disconnected from the financial impact of their decisions.

For example, a global e-commerce company is preparing for Black Friday sales. If they do not know which team is driving the majority of their compute costs or which project is consuming the most storage, they risk overspending without achieving measurable value. Cost allocation bridges this gap by providing a clear breakdown of spending patterns, enabling smarter decision-making, and fostering collaboration between technical and financial teams.

Tagging: The Backbone of Cost Allocation

At the heart of effective cost allocation lies tagging, which is a simple yet powerful tool that transforms raw cloud data into actionable insights. Tags are metadata labels applied to cloud resources, helping categorize them based on attributes such as:

- **Team**: Who owns the resource? (for example, "Marketing," "Engineering")
- **Environment**: Where is it being used? (for example, "Production," "Development," "Testing")
- **Project**: What is it supporting? (for example, "New Website Launch," "Customer Campaign 2024")

Tags provide the context needed to allocate costs accurately. For instance:

- A retail company might tag resources by region (for example, "North America," "Europe") to track regional spending and optimize budgets accordingly

- A SaaS provider could tag resources by customer account to calculate the cost per user, ensuring profitability for each client

Without tagging, cloud costs remain a black box as teams provision resources without understanding their financial impact, leading to wasted budgets and unused assets.

Designing an Effective Tagging Strategy

A well-designed tagging strategy is consistent, mandatory, and aligned with business goals. Here is how to create one that works:

- **Define Tagging Standards:** Start by deciding which tags are required and which are optional. Commonly required tags include:
    - **Owner**: Identifies who is responsible for the resource (for example, "HR_Department").
    - **Environment**: Specifies the purpose of the resource (for example, "Production," "Development").
    - **Project**: Links the resource to a specific initiative (for example, "Q4 Marketing Campaign").
- Use simple, descriptive names that everyone understands. Avoid jargon or overly complex naming conventions that could confuse users.
- **Enforce Compliance:** Tags are only effective if they are consistently applied. To ensure compliance:
    - Make tagging mandatory for all new resources through governance policies.
    - Automate enforcement: a tool such as Cloud Custodian can help to enforce and make this mandatory. AWS Service Control Policies (SCPs) or Azure Policy, which prevent untagged resources from being deployed.
- **Monitor and Audit:** Regularly review tagging compliance to identify gaps and address inconsistencies. Tools such as AWS Config or Azure Monitor can help automate audits, flagging resources that lack required tags.

Common Mistakes in Tagging

Even with the best intentions, organizations often stumble when implementing tagging strategies. Here are some common pitfalls and how to avoid them:

- **Inconsistent Naming Conventions:** Using different terms for the same attribute (for example, "Prod" versus "Production") creates confusion and makes it harder to consolidate data.

Solution: Standardize naming conventions across the organization and document them in a shared tagging policy.

- **Lack of Enforcement:** If tagging is optional, teams may skip it altogether, leaving resources unattributed.

  Solution: Enforce tagging through automation and governance policies. For example, AWS allows you to deny resource creation unless specific tags are applied.

- **Overcomplicating Tags:** Too many tags can overwhelm users and dilute their effectiveness. For instance, requiring 10+ tags for every resource may lead to resistance or errors.

  Solution: Focus on a small set of high-impact tags that align with your organization's priorities. Expand gradually as needed.

Case Study: UST Helps Telecom Giant Cut Cloud Costs with Tagging

Challenge: A major telecom company struggled with over 84,000 untagged AWS resources, resulting in limited visibility and rapidly increasing cloud expenses.

Solution: UST implemented a comprehensive and automated tagging strategy, organizing cloud resources by team, project, environment, and region. This improved transparency, enabled accurate cost allocation, and reduced waste.

Results:

- **80% cost reduction** on previously untagged resources (~$1 million/year)
- **3,000 unused resources** removed, saving an additional $118,000
- Strengthened cost governance and accountability across teams[3]

Advanced Cost Allocation Techniques

While tagging is the foundation of cost allocation, organizations can take it a step further with advanced techniques. A mature FinOps practice requires clear systems for cost accountability. The two primary models for this are chargeback and showback. These approaches formalize financial responsibility for cloud spending across business units.

[3] UST improved cost efficiency for a telecom client by implementing tagging, automation, and chargeback–reducing waste and enhancing team accountability. Source: UST

- **Chargeback and Showback Models**
  - **Chargeback:** Directly billing teams or departments for their cloud usage. This model encourages accountability but can be politically sensitive.
  - **Showback:** Sharing cost reports with teams without charging them directly. This approach fosters transparency without creating friction.

  For example, a SaaS provider might use a showback model to demonstrate how much each product line contributes to overall cloud costs, enabling better alignment with revenue goals.

- **Cost Per Unit Metrics:** Breaking down costs into granular metrics, such as cost per transaction, cost per user, or cost per API call, provides deeper insights into efficiency. **Example**: An e-commerce platform calculates the cost per order processed during peak sales periods, helping them optimize resource allocation.

Dynamic Allocation: Some organizations use machine learning tools to allocate costs dynamically based on usage patterns. For instance, AWS Cost Explorer can automatically categorize spending by service, region, or tag, reducing manual effort.

The Ripple Effect of Effective Cost Allocation

When done right, cost allocation and tagging drive benefits that extend far beyond cost savings:

- **Improved Collaboration:** Breaking down silos between finance, engineering, and leadership fosters trust and alignment. Teams work together to balance innovation with fiscal discipline.
- **Faster Decision-Making:** Real-time visibility enables quicker responses to changing market conditions. For example, an e-commerce company can scale resources dynamically during Black Friday sales without overspending.
- **Sustainability Goals:** Reducing cloud waste is not just economical–it is ecological. A single unused server emits 2.5 tons of CO_2 annually. By optimizing resources, companies such as Etsy have cut energy consumption by 15%, supporting their net-zero pledges.

Turning Chaos into Clarity

Cost allocation and tagging are the cornerstones of effective cloud financial management. By assigning ownership, enforcing compliance, and leveraging advanced techniques such as chargeback models and dynamic allocation, organizations can turn raw data into actionable insights.

This disciplined approach transforms cloud financial management from an operational burden into a core component of business strategy and competitive advantage.

Creating Visibility for Stakeholders Through Reporting

Reporting is the bridge that transforms raw, complex cloud cost data into actionable insights. It goes beyond simply presenting numbers and crafts an understandable story that stakeholders can act upon. Whether you are addressing executives focused on strategic decisions, finance teams managing budgets, or engineers optimizing resources, effective reporting ensures everyone is aligned and working toward shared objectives.

At the heart of this process are key report types such as chargeback and showback, that provide tailored views of cloud spending. Chargeback allocates costs directly to the teams or departments responsible for consumption, reinforcing accountability. Showback provides visibility into usage and spending trends without direct financial attribution, fostering awareness and informed decision-making.

Without clear and concise reporting, cloud cost data remains abstract and difficult to interpret. Reporting demystifies this data, turning it into a powerful tool for driving accountability, transparency, and cross-functional collaboration across teams.

[This topic aligns with Exam Domain 2: Cloud Cost Visibility, which emphasizes the importance of reporting, chargeback/showback models, and delivering actionable financial insights across teams.]

Key Elements of Cloud Cost Reports

Mastering cloud financial management requires moving beyond raw data to generate actionable business intelligence. The consistent creation and analysis of standardized cost reports forms the critical bridge between technical expenditure and strategic decision-making. These reports transform vast, complex streams of billing data into a clear, coherent narrative, enabling stakeholders across finance, engineering, and leadership to understand spending trends, pinpoint optimization opportunities, and align cloud investments with overarching business objectives. Ultimately, a disciplined reporting practice is what turns visibility into control and data into value.

- **Cost Breakdowns:** Breaking down costs by category provides a clear picture of where money is being spent. For example:
  - **Compute**: 60% of costs might come from running virtual machines
  - **Storage**: 20% could be tied to storing backups or customer data
  - **Networking**: 10% may be attributed to data transfer fees
  - **Other**: The remaining 10% could include services such as AI/ML tools or monitoring solutions

  Example: A retail company analyzing its cloud spending discovers that compute instances account for the majority of its costs. By identifying this trend, they can explore optimization strategies such as rightsizing or switching to reserved instances.

- **Trend Analysis:** Tracking changes in spending over time helps identify patterns and anomalies. For instance:
  - A sudden spike in costs during the holiday season might indicate increased traffic due to seasonal promotions.
  - A gradual increase in storage costs could signal inefficient data management practices.

  Example: An e-commerce platform notices a consistent rise in networking costs over three months. Upon investigation, they discovered redundant API calls consuming bandwidth and implementing caching solutions to reduce expenses.

- **Forecasting:** Predicting future spending based on historical data enables proactive decision-making. Forecasting helps organizations anticipate budget overruns and take corrective action before costs spiral out of control.

  Example: A SaaS provider forecasts that their annual cloud costs will exceed the allocated budget unless they optimize resource usage. Armed with this insight, they prioritize initiatives such as decommissioning unused servers and consolidating storage.

Tools for Reporting Cloud Native Tools

Cloud providers offer built-in tools that make it easy to track spending without leaving their platforms. These tools are straightforward, integrated, and give teams a solid starting point for understanding cloud costs.

Some popular examples include:

- **AWS Cost Explorer:** Offers detailed breakdowns of AWS spending, with trend analysis and forecasting

- **Azure Cost Management:** Provides dashboards, budget tracking, and alerts tailored for Azure environments
- **Google Cloud Billing:** Helps visualize usage patterns, detect anomalies, and monitor spending across Google Cloud services

These native tools are free and tightly integrated with their respective platforms, making them great for getting quick insights. However, they are typically limited to single-cloud views and may lack the advanced features needed for more complex or multi-cloud environments.[4]

Third-Party Tools

When you are managing cloud costs across multiple platforms, native tools can only take you so far. That is where third-party solutions come in. Tools such as **CloudHealth**, **Apptio Cloudability**, and **Spot.io** offer more flexibility, with features such as customizable dashboards, in-depth analytics, and automation that help teams spot and act on cost-saving opportunities faster.

These platforms are especially helpful in multi-cloud environments, where visibility can easily get fragmented. Although they require an investment of time and budget to get started, better insights and smarter decisions can pay significant dividends in the long run.[5]

Business Intelligence (BI) Tools

For teams that want to go beyond basic dashboards, **Business Intelligence (BI) tools** such as **Tableau** and **Power BI** offer powerful ways to explore and visualize cloud cost data. These platforms connect directly to cloud data sources, allowing you to build custom dashboards, uncover patterns, and tell a clearer story with numbers.

They are especially useful when you need to share insights with non-technical stakeholders in a more engaging, visual way. Just keep in mind that you might require some technical knowledge to set them up, connect data sources, and maintain them over time.[6]

---

[4] Native tools like AWS Cost Explorer, Azure Cost Management, and Google Cloud Billing offer basic cost visibility within each cloud provider. finops.org

[5] Third-party tools like CloudHealth, Apptio, and Spot.io offer advanced analytics and multi-cloud visibility beyond native tooling. finops.org

[6] BI tools such as Tableau and Power BI enable advanced cloud cost visualization and storytelling, though they require technical setup. finops.org

Best Practices for Reporting

- **Tailor Reports to Your Audience:** Different stakeholders have different needs which are mentioned as follows:
    - Executives prefer high-level summaries, focusing on overall trends and ROI.
    - Finance Teams need detailed breakdowns to reconcile budgets and track spending.
    - Engineers require granular insights to identify inefficiencies, and optimize resources.
- **Use Visuals such as Charts and Graphs:** Visual aids simplify complex data, making it easier to digest. For example:
    - Use bar charts to compare spending across departments
    - Use line graphs to show monthly trends
    - Use pie charts to illustrate cost breakdowns by category
- **Schedule Regular Reviews:** Consistent communication keeps stakeholders informed and engaged. Weekly or monthly reviews ensure the timely identification of issues and opportunities.

  Example: A logistics company conducts monthly reviews to analyze cloud spending trends. During one session, they notice a recurring spike in storage costs and decide to implement lifecycle policies to delete stale data.

Setting Up Cost Visibility Tools

Accurate cloud expenditure visibility requires specialized tools and processes, aligning technology, people, and procedures. Proper configuration and integration are crucial to transform raw billing data into a reliable single source of truth for cost optimization and strategic planning.

Choosing the Right Tools

Selecting the right tools depends on your organization's size, complexity, and cloud strategy. Here is a quick comparison of a few of them:

Tool Type	Pros	Cons
Native Cloud Tools	Free, integrated with cloud providers	Limited to single-cloud environments
Third-Party Tools	Multi-cloud support, advanced analytics	Can be expensive

Custom Solutions	Fully customizable	Requires development effort

***Table 3.1**: Comparison of FinOps Tool Categories*

This table provides a comparative overview of different types of FinOps tools, highlighting their advantages and limitations to help organizations select the right solution based on their specific needs.

Steps to Set Up Cost Visibility

Implementing an effective cost visibility framework is a systematic process that involves careful planning and execution across several key phases.

1. **Identify Key Metrics:** Focus on the metrics that matter most to your business. Examples include:
    - Cost per user
    - Cost per API call
    - Monthly spend versus budget
    - Integrate Data Sources
    - Pull data from all relevant cloud accounts and tools to create a unified view of spending
2. **Build Dashboards:** Create dashboards that highlight key insights and trends. Use visuals such as charts, graphs, and heatmaps to make data engaging and accessible
3. **Set Alerts:** Configure alerts for unexpected spikes or budget overruns. Real-time notifications help teams respond quickly to anomalies

Recommended Approach: Achieving Comprehensive Cloud Cost Visibility

To gain end-to-end visibility and control over cloud spending, organizations can adopt a multi-tool strategy that combines native cloud features with third-party analytics solutions:

- **Use AWS Cost Explorer** to track daily spend and quickly detect cost anomalies
- **Integrate data into visualization tools like Tableau** to build executive-level dashboards highlighting monthly trends, forecasts, and KPIs
- **Set up automated budget alerts** to flag overspending in real time, enabling prompt corrective actions

By combining these practices, organizations can improve financial accountability, uncover inefficiencies, and realize significant savings that can **often reduce cloud costs by up to 25% within six months** through proactive optimization.

The Ripple Effect of Effective Reporting

When done right, reporting drives benefits that extend far beyond cost savings:

- **Improved Collaboration:** Breaking down silos between finance, engineering, and leadership fosters trust and alignment. Teams work together to balance innovation with fiscal discipline.
- **Faster Decision-Making:** Real-time visibility enables quicker responses to changing market conditions. For example, an e-commerce company can scale resources dynamically during Black Friday sales without overspending.
- **Sustainability Goals:** Organizations can achieve their respective ecological and economical goals by reducing cloud waste. A single unused server emits 2.5 tons of CO_2 annually. By optimizing resources, companies such as Etsy have cut energy consumption by 15% and have supported their net-zero pledges.

Turning Data into Action

Effective reporting is the cornerstone of FinOps' success. By transforming raw data into actionable insights, organizations can foster accountability, transparency, and collaboration.

Embracing these principles can help businesses navigate the complexities of the digital age with confidence and achieve both financial and operational excellence.

Communicating Insights to Stakeholders: Bridging the Gap between Data and Action

When it comes to cloud cost management, effective communication is key to driving alignment and action. However, not all stakeholders are the same—they have different priorities, concerns, and levels of technical expertise. Understanding who these stakeholders are and what they care about is the first step in crafting meaningful insights.

- **Executives:** Executives are focused on the big picture. They care about overall spending, return on investment (ROI), and how cloud costs align with strategic business goals. For them, the emphasis is on high-level summaries that highlight trends, risks, and opportunities for improvement.

- **Finance Teams:** Finance teams are the gatekeepers of budgets and forecasts. They need detailed breakdowns of spending, compliance reports, and projections to ensure financial health. Their focus is on accuracy, accountability, and ensuring that cloud investments deliver measurable value.
- **Engineering Teams:** Engineers are the ones provisioning and managing cloud resources. They need granular data and actionable recommendations to optimize resource usage without compromising performance. For them, insights should be practical and tied to specific actions, such as shutting down unused instances or right-sizing overprovisioned servers.

Tailoring Communication for Stakeholder Needs

One size does not fit all when it comes to communicating cloud cost insights. To ensure your message resonates, tailor your approach to each stakeholder group:

- **For Executives: High-Level Summaries with Visual Impact**

  Executives do not have time to sift through granular data as they need concise, visually compelling summaries that tell a clear story. Use visuals such as bar charts, trend lines, and pie charts to highlight key metrics such as total spending, year-over-year trends, and ROI.

  Recommended approach: To effectively communicate cloud cost improvements to executive stakeholders, consider creating a high-level single-slide dashboard that highlights key metrics. This dashboard should include a trend line illustrating reductions in unnecessary spending, such as cloud waste over time, alongside a bar chart that compares current costs to historical budgets. Presenting a clear and concise visual, such as a 20% reduction in cloud waste over six months, helps demonstrate tangible impact and builds trust in the organization's optimization efforts. By showcasing these results in an accessible format, you can foster executive confidence and secure buy-in for future FinOps initiatives.

- **For Finance Teams: Detailed Breakdowns and Forecasts**

  Finance teams thrive on detail. Provide them with comprehensive reports that break down spending by department, project, or environment. Include forecasts to help them anticipate future costs and adjust budgets accordingly.

  Recommended Approach for Finance Teams: Share monthly cost breakdowns that highlight areas of overspending and include projections based on historical usage data. This enables finance teams to reallocate budgets proactively, make informed adjustments, and avoid unexpected costs at the end of the quarter.

- **For Engineering Teams: Granular Data and Actionable Recommendations**

  Engineers need insights they can act on immediately. Share granular data about resource usage and provide specific recommendations for optimization. For instance, flag unused instances, suggest rightsizing opportunities, or recommend switching to spot instances for non-critical workloads.

  Strategy for Engineering Team: Continuously monitor for idle resources, such as underutilized Elastic Compute Cloud instances, and quantify their cost impact. Share these insights with engineering teams in a timely manner, along with clear recommendations for decommissioning or repurposing. This proactive collaboration can eliminate waste quickly and drive immediate savings.

Case Study: Capital One's Centralized FinOps Team

Capital One recognized early on that effective communication was critical to successful cloud cost management. To address this, they created a centralized FinOps team tasked with gathering, analyzing, and communicating cloud cost insights across departments.

Here is how they tailored their approach:

1. **Executives:** Received high-level dashboards showing overall spending trends and ROI metrics. These visuals highlighted the impact of cost-saving initiatives and aligned cloud investments with strategic goals.
2. **Finance Teams:** Were provided with detailed reports breaking down spending by department and project. The FinOps team also shared forecasts to help finance anticipate future costs and allocate budgets effectively.
3. **Engineering Teams:** Got granular insights into resource usage, along with actionable recommendations for optimization. For example, engineers received alerts about underutilized databases and instructions to resize or decommission them.

Results:

1. **Improved Collaboration:** By tailoring reports to each stakeholder group, Capital One fostered better communication between IT, finance, and leadership teams.
2. **Faster Decision-Making:** Clear, actionable insights enabled quicker responses to cost-saving opportunities, such as scaling resources during peak periods and decommissioning unused assets.

3. **Cost Savings:** Within a year, Capital One achieved a 25% reduction in cloud costs, proving the value of effective communication in driving results[7].

Best Practices for Communicating Insights

Transforming raw cost data into actionable strategy requires a deliberate approach to communication, ensuring that insights lead to informed decisions and organizational alignment.

- **Use Visualizations to Simplify Complex Data:** Charts, graphs, and dashboards make it easier for stakeholders to grasp complex information quickly. For example, use heatmaps to show cost hotspots or trend lines to illustrate spending patterns over time.
- **Leverage Storytelling to Make Data Relatable:** Numbers alone can feel abstract. Frame your insights as stories that connect the data to real-world outcomes. For instance, instead of saying, "We saved $50,000," say, "By shutting down unused instances, we freed up resources equivalent to powering 100 homes annually."
- **Provide Context for Anomalies:** A sudden spike in costs might raise alarms, but context is crucial. Explain whether the increase was due to legitimate business needs (for example, a marketing campaign) or inefficiencies (for example, overprovisioned resources).
- **Celebrate Wins to Reinforce Positive Behaviors:** Highlight successes–big and small–to motivate teams. For example, recognize an engineering team that reduced database costs by 15% or celebrate hitting a quarterly budget target.

The Ripple Effect of Effective Communication

When insights are communicated effectively, the benefits extend far beyond cost savings:

- **Improved Collaboration:** Breaking down silos between finance, engineering, and leadership fosters trust and alignment. Teams work together to balance innovation with fiscal discipline.
- **Faster Decision-Making:** Real-time visibility enables quicker responses to changing market conditions. For example, an e-commerce company can scale resources dynamically during Black Friday sales without overspending.

---

[7] Capital One's centralized FinOps strategy, which achieved a 25% reduction in cloud costs, has been featured in case studies and presentations by the FinOps Foundation. Source

- **Sustainability Goals:** Reducing cloud waste is not just economical, but also ecological. A single unused server emits 2.5 tons of CO_2 annually. By optimizing resources, companies such as Etsy have cut energy consumption by 15%, supporting their net-zero pledges.

Turning Insights into Action

Communicating insights to stakeholders is more than just sharing data–it is about turning numbers into actionable strategies. By tailoring your approach to each stakeholder group, you can ensure that your message resonates and drives meaningful change.

A core principle of the FinOps Foundation framework is that organizations must "enable informed, timely, and cost-effective decision making." By embracing these principles, businesses can navigate the complexities of the digital age with confidence, achieving both financial and operational excellence.

Conclusion

The Inform phase is the cornerstone of FinOps, providing the visibility needed to manage cloud costs effectively. By gathering accurate data, implementing robust tagging strategies, and creating transparent reports, organizations can empower stakeholders to make informed decisions. This phase sets the stage for optimization and operational excellence, ensuring that every dollar spent on the cloud delivers maximum value.

As cloud environments grow more complex, the importance of the Inform phase will only increase. Organizations that master this phase will be better equipped to navigate the challenges of cloud financial management and achieve long-term success. The next chapter explains the Optimize phase.

Key Terms

- **FinOps:** A framework for managing cloud financial operations, emphasizing collaboration between finance, engineering, and business teams.
- **Inform Phase:** The foundational FinOps phase focused on gathering, analyzing, and communicating cloud cost data for visibility and accountability.
- **Tagging:** Metadata labels applied to cloud resources to categorize costs by team, project, or environment.
- **Chargeback/Showback:** Models for allocating costs (charging teams directly) or sharing cost visibility (without direct billing).

- **Right-Sizing:** Optimizing cloud resources to match workload requirements and avoid overprovisioning.
- **Reserved Instances:** Pre-purchased cloud resources offering cost savings for long-term usage commitments.
- **Data Fragmentation:** Challenges in consolidating cost data across multi-cloud environments.
- **AWS Cost Explorer/Azure Cost Management/Google Cloud Billing:** Native tools for tracking cloud spending.
- **CloudHealth/Apptio:** Third-party tools for multi-cloud cost analytics and governance.
- **Sustainability:** Reducing cloud waste to lower carbon footprint (for example, unused servers emitting CO_2).

Points to Remember

- **Visibility is Critical**: Unchecked cloud spending leads to waste (about 30% to 40% overspending), budget overruns, and accountability gaps
- **Tagging Strategies**: Mandatory, standardized tags (for example, team, environment) enable accurate cost allocation and accountability
- **Tools Matter**: Use native tools (AWS Cost Explorer) for single-cloud and third-party tools (CloudHealth) for multi-cloud visibility
- **Reporting** Tailored to Stakeholders:
  - **Executives**: High-level summaries with visuals
  - **Finance**: Detailed breakdowns and forecasts
  - **Engineers**: Granular optimization recommendations
- **Case Study Outcomes**:
  - **Spotify**: Reduced 35% waste via tagging
  - **Capital One**: Saved 25% costs through centralized FinOps
  - **Dropbox**: Millions saved by deleting stale data
- **Best Practices**: Automate data collection, enforce tagging policies, and set real-time alerts for anomalies

Questions

1. Why is the Inform Phase considered the cornerstone of FinOps?
2. How does tagging address accountability gaps in cloud spending?

3. What are the risks of not enforcing standardized tagging policies?
4. Explain the difference between chargeback and showback models.
5. How can organizations balance cost optimization with sustainability goals?

Multiple Choice Questions

1. What is the primary goal of the Inform Phase?
    a. Reducing cloud usage
    b. Increasing visibility into cloud spending
    c. Migrating to multi-cloud
    d. Improving server performance
2. Which tool is best for multi-cloud cost management?
    a. AWS Cost Explorer
    b. Azure Policy
    c. CloudHealth
    d. Google Cloud Billing
3. Which strategy helped Spotify reduce cloud waste by 35%?
    a. Reserved Instances
    b. Robust tagging strategies
    c. Switching to spot instances
    d. Deleting S3 buckets
4. Which stakeholder group needs granular data on resource usage?
    a. Executives
    b. Finance teams
    c. Engineering teams
    d. Marketing teams

5. What sustainability benefit arises from optimizing cloud resources?
    a. Faster API responses
    b. Reduced CO_2 emissions
    c. Lower data transfer costs
    d. Improved team morale
6. Which practice ensures tagging compliance?
    a. Optional tagging policies
    b. Manual audits
    c. Automation tools like AWS SCPs
    d. Weekly team meetings
7. A sudden spike in cloud costs during Black Friday is an example of:
    a. Data fragmentation
    b. Trend analysis
    c. Budget overrun
    d. Chargeback model

Answers

1. b
2. c
3. b
4. c
5. b
6. c
7. b

CHAPTER 4
Optimize Phase: Cost Allocation Techniques

Introduction

Now that we have laid the groundwork for visibility in the Inform phase, it is time to dig in and take action. The Optimize phase of FinOps is where the rubber meets the road. This is where organizations transform insights into results.

Think of the Optimize phase as the spring cleaning cycle for your cloud environment, which is a time for both renewal and strategic refinement. It is about decluttering unused resources, organizing essential workloads, and ensuring every dollar spent delivers maximum business value.

Imagine opening your garage after years of neglect: old bikes, unused tools, and forgotten holiday decorations. Cleaning it out feels overwhelming at first, but once you begin, you can reclaim space, reduce costs, and restore order. The Optimize phase works in the same way, except that instead of dusty boxes, you are addressing idle servers, overprovisioned databases, and redundant storage. This process goes beyond cleanup; it is a disciplined practice of resource rationalization, cost governance, and performance optimization that transforms technical debt into strategic efficiency. By the end of this chapter, you will have a toolkit to drive efficiency, foster accountability, and turn cloud costs from a liability into a strategic asset.

Structure

In this chapter, we will cover the following topics:

- Rightsizing and Resource Optimization
- Leveraging Reserved Instances and Spot Instances
- Scheduling Workloads for Cost Efficiency
- Identifying and Eliminating Wasted Resources

Resizing and Resource Optimization

Cost allocation is the backbone of the Optimize phase. It is not enough to know *how much* you are spending, you need to know *who* is spending it and *why*. Without clear cost allocation, cloud spending becomes a tangled web of unattributed expenses, which often leaves behind teams in silos and unmet strategic goals.

Consider the example of a company where every department has a shared bank account. The marketing department splurges on ads, engineering teams invest in servers, and product teams experiment with new tools, all without tracking who is responsible for their respective expenses. By month's end, no one knows why the account is empty. These are the chaos many organizations face in cloud cost management when cost allocation is ignored.

The Optimize phase relies on cost allocation to turn this chaos into clarity. It ensures that every cloud dollar is tied to a specific team, project, or outcome, and empowers organizations to align spending with value. When a team's spending is clearly visible, it becomes easier to identify oversized virtual machines running at 10% CPU utilization, or databases with excessive memory allocation. Armed with this insight, cloud architects can rightsize instances, scale down idle resources, and eliminate redundancy, reducing costs without sacrificing performance. In this way, cost allocation does not just track spending, it *enables* technical optimization, which ensures that resources are aligned with actual demand and business value.

The Problem with Unattributed Costs

In the cloud's Pay-As-You-Go model, costs can spiral out of control when left untracked. For example:

- A marketing team might spin up servers for a campaign, assuming "the cloud is cheap".
- Engineers might overprovision databases "just in case," leaving them idle.
- Product teams might test new features but forget to decommission resources afterward.

Without cost allocation, these expenses blend into a murky pool. Finance teams see a bloated bill but cannot pinpoint the source, while technical teams remain unaware of their financial impact.

Such scenarios are like a family sharing a credit card, where everyone spends freely, but no one is actually responsible for the bill.

[This corresponds to Exam Objective 1: FinOps Principles and Framework and Exam Objective 3: Rate Optimization, which emphasizes the need to connect technical metrics

with business outcomes, demonstrate ROI, and ensure that optimization efforts deliver measurable value rather than just cost reduction.]

How Cost Allocation Drives Optimization

Cost allocation techniques such as tagging, chargeback models, and resource ownership clarify this chaos, enabling targeted optimization. These techniques are mentioned as follows:

- **Tagging: The GPS for Cloud Spending**

  Tags act as metadata labels, categorizing resources by team, project, or environment. For example:

  - A retail company tags resources by campaign (for example, "Holiday Sale 2023")
  - A SaaS provider tags resources by customer account to calculate the cost per user

  The Impact of Tagging via a Real-World Example: Spotify used tagging to identify $2 million wasted annually on unused Kubernetes clusters. By assigning ownership to teams, they reduced costs by 35% in 1 year.

- **Chargeback Models: Accountability in Action**

  Chargeback models allocate costs directly to departments or projects, creating a "cost-aware" culture. For example, Netflix ties cloud costs to product teams. If a team launches a recommendation algorithm, it owns its expenses. This practice ensures that every dollar spent aligns with the business outcomes.

- **Resource Ownership: Empowering Teams**

  Assigning ownership ensures teams take responsibility for their resources.

  Case Study: Capital One's engineers began tagging resources consistently, leading to a 25% cost reduction. Fostering ownership increased proactive optimization, such as deleting stale data and rightsizing instances.

The Human Side of Cost Allocation

Cost allocation is not just a technical or financial process, but a cultural shift as it moves organizations away from thinking in silos and propels them towards an environment of shared responsibility.

In many companies, engineers, product managers, and even marketing teams interact with cloud resources daily. Without visibility into costs, teams may unknowingly drive up the cloud spend. However, when costs are clearly attributed to the teams and services generating them, a new mindset rooted in ownership and accountability emerges.

Cost allocation is not about shifting and assigning blame; it is an exercise in empowerment.

When teams see how their decisions impact budgets, they naturally begin to optimize resources and expenditure. Thus, transparency creates trust and trust drives action.

We can see the impact of transparency through the following example:

A prominent example comes from Autodesk, a leader in 3D design and engineering software. The company identified that a large portion of its cloud spend was allocated to underutilized Amazon EC2 instances. By implementing a systematic rightsizing initiative using AWS Cost Explorer and Trusted Advisor, Autodesk's cloud team was able to analyze instance utilization and downsize or terminate inefficient resources. This data-driven approach, which required close collaboration between their finance and engineering departments, resulted in a 40% reduction in their EC2 costs, saving millions of dollars annually while maintaining all critical application performance.[1]

This case demonstrates that precise cost visibility, when paired with collaborative analysis, unlocks optimization opportunities that directly impact the bottom line without compromising operational integrity.

[This supports Exam Objective 1: FinOps Principles and Framework and Exam Objective 2: Cloud Cost Allocation and Accountability by emphasizing how cost allocation promotes a culture of shared responsibility and empowers engineers to make cost-conscious decisions, while aligning cloud usage with business outcomes.]

Common Mistakes in Cost Allocation

Even with the best tools, organizations often encounter the following challenges:

- **Inconsistent Tagging:** Tags such as "Prod" versus "Production" or "TeamA" versus "Marketing" create confusion.

  Solution: Standardize naming conventions and automate enforcement.

- **Lack of Ownership Policies:** Teams provision resources but do not track their usage.

  Solution: Use governance tools (for example AWS SCPs) to enforce ownership.

[1]"AWS Case Study: Autodesk," *Amazon Web Services, Inc.*, https://aws.amazon.com/solutions/case-studies/autodesk-case-study/. The case study specifically notes: "By using AWS services and solutions, Autodesk has been able to reduce its EC2 costs by 40 percent."

- **Ignoring Cultural Resistance:** Teams may push back against accountability.

  Solution: Celebrate wins and involve teams in creating policies.

Real-World Impact: How Dropbox Saved $10 Million

Dropbox[2], a global leader in cloud storage and collaboration tools, faced ballooning cloud costs as their infrastructure scaled. Rather than resorting to blanket cuts, their FinOps team used **granular cost allocation reports** to dig deeper into usage patterns across various teams and services.

During this analysis, they uncovered a surprising insight: over **200 terabytes of data** stored in Amazon S3 buckets were **no longer being accessed**. These were old backups, logs, or files linked to deprecated projects that were accumulating storage costs over time and contributed little to active operations.

By validating this with stakeholders and ensuring no mission-critical data was removed, Dropbox proceeded to **delete the stale data**. The resultant effect saw Dropbox sustain a reduction of **$10 million** in annual cloud spend.

Key Takeaway

Cost allocation is not just about identifying waste–it creates room for innovation by surfacing inefficiencies at a granular level and helping teams make informed decisions that **free up resources**. These reclaimed funds can be later **reinvested into product development, customer experience, or strategic growth**, turning what used to be sunk costs into competitive advantage.

Best Practices for Effective Cost Allocation

Implementing cost allocation is a technical exercise and a strategic endeavor that requires careful planning and cross-organizational alignment to be truly effective.

- **Align Tags with Business Goals:** Use tags that reflect organizational priorities, such as "Customer-Facing" versus "Internal Tools"
- **Combine Chargeback with Education:** Show teams how their spending impacts budgets and train them to optimize
- **Automate Enforcement:** Use tools such as AWS Config or Azure Policy to block untagged resources

[2]Dropbox's broader infrastructure optimization efforts, including S3 storage cleanup, contributed to nearly $75 million in savings over two years. Source: GeekWire – "Dropbox saved almost $75 million in two years by building its own tech infrastructure".

The Ripple Effect of Cost Allocation: When done right, cost allocation transforms organizations in the following ways:

- **Improved Collaboration:** Finance and engineering teams work together to balance budgets and performance
- **Faster Decision-Making:** Teams can act quickly on insights, such as scaling resources during peak demand
- **Sustainability Wins:** Reducing waste lowers carbon footprints—Etsy cut energy use by 15% by eliminating idle resources

From Chaos to Clarity: Cost allocation is the compass guiding the optimization phase. By assigning ownership and clarifying spending patterns, organizations can eliminate waste, align cloud investments with strategic goals, and foster a culture of accountability.

Key Activities in the Optimize Phase

Here is a brief list of the key activities that comprise the Optimize phase:

- Rightsizing compute, storage, and networking resources
- Identifying underutilized services and shutting them down
- Implementing savings plans or reserved instances
- Adjusting autoscaling parameters for efficiency
- Leveraging spot instances or ephemeral resources

Rightsizing: Matching Resources to Reality

Rightsizing is all about aligning cloud resources with actual usage. Overprovisioned resources, such as running a small database on a server built for heavy workloads, are a drain on both budgets and efficiency. By rightsizing, organizations can eliminate waste while maintaining performance.

Real-World Example: Rightsizing at a Healthcare Technology Provider

THNKBIG, a digital transformation partner for healthcare organizations, worked with a U.S.-based provider to modernize its analytics infrastructure using **Azure Kubernetes Service (AKS)**. The provider had been relying on overprovisioned Azure Virtual Machines (VMs) to handle clinical data pipelines and patient analytics workloads. While these static VMs ensured uptime, they also resulted in significant underutilization during off-peak hours.

After reviewing resource metrics, THNKBIG[3] identified an opportunity to optimize cloud spending through **rightsizing**. They migrated the provider's workloads from fixed-size VMs to **containerized workloads on AKS**, enabling more precise allocation of compute resources.

By implementing **cluster auto-scaling**, fine-tuning **pod resource limits**, and leveraging **zero-trust architecture**, the organization not only improved its security posture but also achieved a **25% reduction in cloud infrastructure costs**. These savings were reinvested into patient-facing digital services and expanded analytics capabilities.

Think of it as trading in a gas-guzzling SUV for a fuel-efficient hybrid, which is smarter, leaner, and aligned with real usage patterns under a cloud consumption model.

Best Practices

- Use tools such as **AWS Trusted Advisor**, **Azure Advisor**, or **Google Cloud Recommender** to identify overprovisioned or idle resources.
- Test configuration changes in **staging environments** before applying them to production to ensure stability and avoid outages.
- Set up **automated alerts or schedules** to re-evaluate resource sizing periodically.

Effort vs. Reward Breakdown

To strategically prioritize cloud optimization initiatives, it is essential to evaluate the potential return on investment against the required implementation effort.

Factor	Detail
Effort level	Medium – requires analysis of usage patterns and testing adjustments.
Tools required	AWS Trusted Advisor, Azure Advisor, GCP Recommender, CloudHealth, CloudZero.
Typical cost saving	15%–40% depending on how overprovisioned the environment is.

***Table 4.1**: Rightsizing Initiative - Effort vs. Reward Analysis*

The table provides a practical breakdown of the effort, tools, and potential savings associated with a typical cloud resource rightsizing project.

[3] *This case study is based on the real-world implementation led by THNKBIG and detailed in their official report: Transforming Patient Care with Azure Kubernetes & Zero Trust Security*

Reserved Instances: Committing to Savings

Reserved instances allow organizations to lock in significant discounts–up to 72% compared to on-demand pricing, but they require a dedicated commitment. This approach is ideal for predictable, long-term workloads.

For example: A streaming service committed to reserved instances for its video transcoding workloads, saving $2 million annually. It is like signing up for a gym membership instead of paying per visit , where you save more when you know you will use it consistently.

Challenges for Technical Team

Accurate forecasting presents a unique challenge for technical teams, as it requires translating variable development pipelines and unpredictable business demand into reliable financial projections. To mitigate risk:

- Start with short-term commitments (for example 1-year reservations) and monitor utilization closely
- Use predictive analytics tools to make informed decisions about resource needs

Spot Instances: Bargain Hunting in the Cloud

Spot instances let you bid on unused cloud capacity at steep discounts such as ones that are often up to 90% off on-demand prices. These are perfect for non-critical, flexible tasks such as batch processing, data analysis, or machine learning model training.

Use Case: An AI startup used spot instances to train its machine learning models, slashing compute costs by 65%. It is like snagging a last-minute hotel deal for a weekend getaway, which means that you get what you need at a fraction of the cost.

Best Practices

- Combine spot instances with on-demand instances to balance cost savings and reliability
- Implement robust monitoring and auto-scaling policies to ensure critical workloads are not interrupted during peak demand periods

Workload Scheduling: Timing Matters

Aligning resource usage with demand cycles can lead to significant savings. For example, scheduling non-urgent tasks such as batch processing or data backups during off-peak hours, when spot instance prices are lower, can reduce costs without impacting performance.

Impact

A logistics company scheduled its data processing jobs overnight, saving 18% on compute costs. It is like avoiding rush-hour traffic to save time and fuel—timing is everything.

Tips for Success

Use auto-scaling policies to dynamically adjust resources based on demand

- *Leverage tools such as Kubernetes or AWS Lambda for workload orchestration and management*

Identifying Wasted Resources: The Zombie Hunt

Idle instances, orphaned storage, and unused licenses are the "zombies" of the cloud as they consume resources without delivering value. Identifying and eliminating these inefficiencies is a quick win for cost optimization.

Case Study

SaaS provider identified 150TB of stale data and shut down idle servers, saving $75,000 monthly. It is like decluttering your attic and freeing up space while reducing unnecessary expenses.

How to Get Started

- Conduct regular audits to identify unused or underutilized resources
- Automate cleanup processes using scripts or lifecycle policies (for example, AWS S3 lifecycle rules)
- Celebrate wins—big and small—to reinforce positive behaviors across teams

The Ripple Effect of Optimization

When done effectively, optimization creates a ripple effect that extends beyond cost savings:

- **Strengthened Organizational Cohesion**: The process of optimization inherently breaks down traditional barriers, creating a shared language and purpose between finance, engineering, and product teams. This cultivates a culture of mutual ownership where technical and financial health are seen as interconnected goals, not competing priorities.

- **Enhanced Strategic Agility**: With a finely-tuned and cost-aware infrastructure, organizations gain the ability to pivot rapidly. A media streaming service, for instance, can confidently deploy a new, data-intensive feature for a hit show, knowing the underlying architecture can scale efficiently to meet viewer demand without financial surprise.
- **Tangible Sustainability Impact**: The reduction of idle and over-provisioned resources directly translates into a lower carbon footprint from data centers. For example, Capital One optimized its data processing pipelines by migrating from on-premise data centers to AWS and implementing automated scaling. This initiative not only supported their cloud-first strategy but also contributed to a significant reduction in their carbon footprint, aligning with their public commitment to carbon neutrality.[14]

The Human Side of Optimization

Optimization is not just about tweaking servers or crunching numbers. At its core, it is about fostering a sense of ownership and accountability across teams. When teams are empowered and own up to costs, it sets up a precedent for accountability and encourages proactive financial stewardship for their cloud spending. It also motivates teams to make smarter, cost-conscious decisions. This cultural shift transforms optimization from a technical task into a shared mission that drives collaboration, innovation, and continuous improvement.

Collaboration: Bridging the Gap between Teams

One of the most powerful outcomes of optimization is breaking down silos between finance, engineering, and leadership teams. Traditionally, these groups operate in isolation; finance focuses on budgets while engineers prioritize performance and scalability. But in the FinOps world, collaboration becomes the secret sauce for success.

For example, a marketing campaign requires additional cloud resources. Instead of simply provisioning servers without considering costs, the engineering and finance teams work together to strike the right balance. Finance provides insights into budget constraints, while engineering ensures that resource allocation meets technical

---

[4]Capital One's Cloud Journey and Carbon Reduction," *Capital One Tech*, https://www.capitalone.com/tech/cloud/cloud-journey-carbon-reduction/. This article details the company's public commitment and how their cloud migration, including workload optimization, directly supports their sustainability goals.

requirements. This partnership ensures that every dollar spent delivers measurable value.

Celebrating Wins: Reinforcing Positive Behaviors

Recognition plays a crucial role in embedding optimization into an organization's culture. Celebrating wins–whether they are big and small–reinforces positive behaviors and motivates teams to continue improving.

Take, for instance, a developer group that has reduced their database expenses by 30% through rightsizing and lifecycle management. Recognizing this achievement not only boosts morale but also inspires other teams to follow suit. Whether it is a shout-out in a company-wide meeting, a feature in the internal newsletter, or even a small reward, acknowledging these efforts creates a ripple effect of accountability and enthusiasm.

Real-World Example: A SaaS provider celebrated a team that identified and deleted 150TB of stale data, saving $75,000 per month. The recognition did not just highlight their financial impact, but showcased how their actions aligned with the company's sustainability goals and further reinforced the importance of optimization.

Empowering Teams Through Ownership

Ownership is a cornerstone of the human side of optimization. When teams are given responsibility for their cloud spending, they naturally become more mindful of resource usage. For example:

- A product owner might track the cost per transaction for their e-commerce platform, identifying inefficiencies in database queries and working with engineers to optimize performance.
- A cloud engineer might tag Kubernetes clusters and integrate cost data into sprint reviews, turning optimization into a regular part of their workflow.

This sense of ownership fosters a proactive mindset. Teams do not wait for audits or alerts; they actively seek out opportunities to save costs and improve efficiency.

The Ripple Effect of Cultural Change

When organizations prioritize collaboration, celebrate wins, and empower teams, the benefits extend far beyond cost savings:

Sustainability Goals Optimizing cloud operations can yield both financial and environmental benefits. Microsoft has studied how innovations in data center cooling–such as cold plates and immersion systems–can reduce greenhouse gas emissions by 15–21%. This demonstrates how infrastructure-level efficiencies in cloud environments contribute meaningfully to sustainability.[5]

Faster Decision-Making Real-time visibility into application performance and cloud costs enables faster, data-driven responses to changing market conditions. Platforms like **MongoDB Atlas** empower organizations to automatically rightsize their cloud clusters using built-in monitoring and auto-scaling tools–ensuring performance stability while avoiding unnecessary spending.[6]

Turning Optimization Into a Mindset

The human side of optimization does more than cutting costs, as it creates a culture where every decision adds value. By fostering collaboration, celebrating wins, and empowering teams to take ownership, organizations can turn optimization into a sustainable, ongoing practice.

In other words, *FinOps is not just about managing costs; it creates a mindset where every decision adds value. When you get it right, the possibilities are endless.*

Challenges in the Optimize Phase: Navigating Roadblocks to Success

The Optimize phase of FinOps is where the real work begins but it is not without its hurdles. While the goal is to eliminate waste and maximize value, organizations often face resistance, complexity, and have to balance their actions. Let us unpack these challenges and explore how to overcome them with real-world strategies.

Resistance to Change: "But This Is How We Have Always Done It!"

A significant hurdle in any FinOps transformation is overcoming the entrenched mindset of "But this is how we have always done it!" which often serves as the primary barrier to adopting new, more efficient cloud financial practices.

The Problem: Teams may push back against optimization efforts, especially when changes impact their workflows. For example, engineers might resist rightsizing

---

[5] "Microsoft quantifies environmental impacts of data center cooling from cradle to grave in new Nature study," Microsoft News, https://news.microsoft.com/source/features/sustainability/microsoft-data-center-cooling-nature-study/

[6] MongoDB Documentation. *Cluster Auto-Scaling*. MongoDB, Inc. Available at: https://www.mongodb.com/docs/atlas/cluster-autoscaling/ *(Explains how Atlas enables automated, cost-efficient scaling for performance stability.)*

servers if they fear downtime or performance degradation. Similarly, product teams might cling to overprovisioned resources "just to be safe."

Real-World Analogy: Imagine convincing a chef to switch from gas to electric stoves mid-service. Even if the electric stove is cheaper and safer, resistance is natural when people are used to old habits.

Solution:

- **Demonstrate Performance Benefits:** Show teams how optimization improves efficiency. For instance, rightsizing a database might not just save money; it could also reduce latency
- **Involve Teams in Decision-Making:** Collaborate with engineers to test changes in non-production environments. Use A/B testing to prove that optimized resources perform just as well (or better)
- **Celebrate Early Wins:** Highlight successes to build momentum. For example, a retail company celebrated a 20% cost reduction after rightsizing, reinforcing the value of optimization

Example: A gaming startup faced resistance by its own teams when it proposed using spot instances for non-critical workloads. By demonstrating how spot instances could handle batch processing without affecting gameplay, they reduced compute costs by 45% and won team buy-in.

Complexity of Multi-Cloud Environments: Juggling Multiple Balls

Managing costs across multiple cloud providers exponentially increases operational complexity, creating an environment where financial oversight can easily fragment without a unified strategy.

The Problem: Managing costs across AWS, Azure, and Google Cloud introduces complexity. Each platform has its pricing model, tools, and reporting formats. Without a unified view, teams struggle to allocate costs effectively.

Real-World Scenario: A media company using AWS for storage, Azure for analytics, and GCP for Machine Learning, found that its data was highly fragmented. As a result, finance teams spent hours reconciling invoices, while engineers lacked visibility into cross-cloud spending.

Solution:

- **Third-Party Tools:** Platforms such as CloudHealth or Apptio unify data from multiple clouds, simplifying allocation and reporting

- **Standardize Tagging:** Use consistent tags (for example, "Environment: Production") across all cloud providers to track spending holistically
- **Centralized Dashboards:** Create a single source of truth using tools such as Tableau or Grafana to visualize multi-cloud costs

Case Study: Consolidating Multi-Cloud Costs with CloudHealth

A global fintech company operating across multiple markets like North America, Europe, and Southeast Asia faced growing complexity in managing its cloud costs across AWS, Microsoft Azure, and Google Cloud Platform (GCP). Each cloud provider presented siloed billing data, making it difficult for finance and engineering teams to track spending, enforce governance, and identify cost-saving opportunities.

To address this challenge, the firm adopted CloudHealth[7] by VMware, a multi-cloud management platform designed to centralize visibility, optimize resource usage, and drive accountability through tag-based reporting and policy automation.

By aggregating cloud billing data into a single pane of glass, CloudHealth enabled the company to:

- Detect and decommission redundant or idle resources
- Identify oversized compute instances and right-size them
- Track cloud usage by department and business unit via automated tagging
- Enforce policies to prevent unnecessary provisioning

Within the first 12 months of adoption, the organization saved about $1.2 million annually, which was achieved through a mix of optimization, governance enforcement, and improved financial visibility. This efficiency gain allowed them to reallocate cloud budgets toward innovation, improve collaboration between finance and engineering, and accelerate their FinOps maturity journey.

Balancing Savings and Performance: Walking the Tightrope

The most critical and ongoing challenge in cloud optimization is maintaining perfect equilibrium between aggressive cost-saving measures and the unwavering performance requirements of business-critical applications.

---

[7] This case study is a fictionalized example inspired by real-world use cases of CloudHealth. For reference on CloudHealth's capabilities and enterprise adoption, see VMware's case study overview: https://www.vmware.com/docs/case-study-cloudhealth-and-vmware

The Problem: Aggressive optimization can backfire. For example, downsizing servers might save money but lead to slower application performance during peak traffic. Similarly, relying too heavily on spot instances could risk interruptions for critical workloads.

Real-World Analogy: It is like tuning a guitar; if you tighten the strings too much, they snap; too little, and the sound suffers. Finding the right balance is key.

Solution:

- **Monitoring Tools:** Use tools such as AWS CloudWatch or Azure Monitor to track performance metrics alongside costs
- **Set Thresholds:** Define acceptable performance levels (for example, latency under 200ms) before implementing cost-saving measures
- **Gradual Implementation:** Roll out changes incrementally. For instance, start with non-critical workloads when testing spot instances

Example: A streaming service reduced compute costs by 30% by rightsizing instances—without affecting video quality. They used monitoring tools to ensure performance stayed consistent.

Forecasting Uncertainty: Predicting the Unpredictable

Accurately predicting future cloud spend remains notoriously difficult, as it requires translating variable development pipelines and unpredictable business demand into reliable financial projections.

The Problem: Reserved instances require long-term commitments, but forecasting future usage can feel like predicting the weather rather abstractly. Usage patterns shift, and teams may overcommit or underutilize reserved capacity.

Real-World Scenario: A healthcare organization committed to reserved instances for a machine learning project, only to see usage drop by 40% when the project pivoted. The reserved instances sat idle, negating the savings.

Solution:

- **Leverage Predictive Analytics**: Tools such as AWS Cost Explorer or Azure Cost Management use historical data to predict future needs
- **Short-Term Commitments**: Start with 1-year reserved instances instead of 3-year terms to reduce risk
- **Hybrid Models**: Combine reserved instances with on-demand or spot instances to maintain flexibility

Best Practice: A SaaS provider used predictive analytics to forecast usage for their AI workloads, achieving 25% savings on reserved instances without over-committing.

Data Overload: Too Much Noise, Not Enough Signal

A common barrier to effective cloud cost management is data overload, where teams are inundated with raw metrics and alerts but lack the curated, actionable insights needed to make informed financial decisions.

The Problem: Cloud cost reports can overwhelm teams with granular details. Without context, it is hard to prioritize actions.

Solution:

- **Tailor Reports:** Create role-specific dashboards. Executives get high-level summaries, while engineers see actionable insights.
- **Automate Alerts:** Use tools such as PagerDuty or Slack integrations to flag anomalies (for example "Storage costs up 15% this week").
- **Focus on High-Impact Areas:** Prioritize resources that consume the most budget (for example databases, compute clusters).

Case Study: Verizon's Cloud Storage Optimization

Verizon implemented automated monitoring and cleanup of unused cloud resources across their AWS environment. Using AWS Systems Manager and custom automation scripts, the company identified and eliminated over 10 petabytes of unattached EBS volumes and outdated S3 objects. This initiative contributed to Verizon's broader cloud cost optimization program that helped them achieve $100 million in annual savings while improving their operational efficiency.[8]

Cultural Silos: When Teams Do Not Communicate

A fundamental obstacle to FinOps success is the presence of cultural silos, where segregated teams operate with independent goals and limited communication, preventing the unified effort required to align cloud spending with business value.

The Problem: Finance and engineering teams often speak different languages. Finance

[8] "AWS and Verizon Case Study," *Amazon Web Services, Inc.*, https://aws.amazon.com/solutions/case-studies/verizon-case-study/

sees "EC2 Instances," while engineers see "the backbone of our app." This fundamental disconnect often leads to friction.

Solution:

- **Shared Language:** Educate finance teams on technical terms and engineers on budget constraints
- **Regular Sync-Ups:** Hold monthly meetings where both teams review cost and performance data together
- **Showback Models:** Share cost data with teams to foster accountability without direct billing

Real-World Lessons: Overcoming Challenges

Examining how leading enterprises have successfully navigated FinOps challenges provides a practical blueprint for implementing effective solutions.

Case Study: Verizon's Cloud Cost Optimization

Verizon successfully implemented a comprehensive cloud cost optimization program that addressed several key challenges.[9]

- **Resistance to Change**: Teams were accustomed to traditional infrastructure management approaches.

  Solution: Verizon established cloud centers of excellence and provided extensive training on cloud financial management.

- **Multi-Cloud Complexity**: Managed resources across multiple cloud environments while maintaining operational efficiency.

  Solution: Implemented unified cloud management platforms for consistent visibility and control.

- **Balancing Savings/Performance**: Needed to optimize costs without impacting customer-facing services.

  Solution: Deployed automated scaling and rightsizing while maintaining performance standards.

Result: Verizon achieved $100 million in annual cloud savings while improving operational efficiency and maintaining service quality.

---

[9] "AWS and Verizon Case Study," *Amazon Web Services, Inc.*, https://aws.amazon.com/solutions/case-studies/verizon-case-study/

Conclusion

Optimize phase, turning Challenges into Opportunities.

The Optimize phase is riddled with challenges, but they're are not insurmountable. By addressing resistance with empathy, simplifying multi-cloud complexity with tools, and balancing savings with performance monitoring, organizations can transform roadblocks into opportunities.

As one FinOps leader put it: "*Optimization isn't not about cutting—it is about crafting. When you navigate the challenges, you build something stronger.*"

With FinOps, the sky is the limit—literally.

In this chapter, we will deep dive into the Operate phase.

Key Terms

- **Cost Allocation:** The process of attributing cloud spending to specific teams, projects, departments, or business units to enable accountability and informed decision-making.
- **Tagging:** Use of metadata labels (for example, Team: Marketing, Environment: Production) to categorize cloud resources for cost tracking and governance.
- **Chargeback Model:** A cost allocation method where cloud expenses are directly billed to the consuming department or team, promoting financial ownership.
- **Showback Model:** A cost allocation method where teams receive visibility into their cloud spending without direct billing, encouraging cost awareness.
- **Rightsizing:** Adjusting cloud resources (compute, storage, etc.) to match actual workload demands, eliminating overprovisioning and reducing costs.
- **Reserved Instances (RIs):** Prepaid compute capacity commitments (for example, 1 or 3 years) that offer significant discounts (up to 72%) compared to on-demand pricing.
- **Spot Instances:** Low-cost, interruptible compute instances that allow bidding on unused cloud capacity, often at up to 90% discount. Ideal for fault-tolerant, non-critical workloads.
- **Workload Scheduling:** Running non-critical tasks during off-peak hours or when spot prices are low to reduce costs.
- **Wasted Resources (Zombie Resources):** Idle or unused cloud assets (for example, unattached storage, stale databases, orphaned VMs) that incur costs without delivering value.

- **Resource Ownership:** Assigning accountability for cloud resources to specific teams or individuals to drive proactive optimization.
- **FinOps Principles:** A framework combining financial accountability with cloud engineering to optimize cloud spend and drive business value.
- **Predictive Analytics:** Tools and techniques that use historical usage data to forecast future resource needs, aiding in RI planning and capacity management.
- **Multi-Cloud Complexity:** Challenges in managing cost, visibility, and governance across multiple cloud providers (for example, AWS, Azure, GCP).
- **Sustainability in Cloud:** Reducing cloud waste also lowers energy consumption and carbon footprint (for example, one idle server emits ~2.5 tons of CO_2/year).

Points to Remember

- Cost allocation is the backbone of the Optimize phase as it transforms unattributed spending into actionable insights.
- Without cost allocation, cloud spending becomes a "shared credit card" problem–everyone spends, no one takes responsibility.
- Tagging must be consistent since inconsistent tags (for example, "Prod" vs "Production") create confusion and break reporting.
- Chargeback and Showback models foster a cost-aware culture, but require education and collaboration to avoid resistance.
- Rightsizing can yield 20–35% savings without impacting performance; use tools like AWS Trusted Advisor or Azure Advisor.
- Reserved Instances offer deep discounts but require accurate forecasting–start with 1-year terms and use predictive analytics.
- Spot instances are ideal for batch jobs, ML training, and CI/CD pipelines–combine with on-demand instances for reliability.
- Workload scheduling (for example, running jobs at night) can save up to 18% by leveraging lower demand periods.
- Zombie resources (idle VMs, stale data) are low-hanging fruit; regular audits and automation (for example, S3 lifecycle rules) help eliminate them.
- Cultural change is critical as optimization is not just technical; it requires collaboration, ownership, and celebration of wins.
- Multi-cloud environments require unified tools; platforms such as CloudHealth or Apptio provide a single pane of glass for cost visibility.

- Balance cost savings with performance; monitor metrics (for example, latency, error rates) to avoid over-optimization.

Questions

1. Why is cost allocation considered the "compass" of the Optimize phase?
2. How can inconsistent tagging undermine an organization's FinOps efforts?
3. What are the key differences between chargeback and showback models? When might each be appropriate?
4. How does rightsizing contribute to both cost savings and performance improvements?
5. What are the risks of over-relying on reserved instances? How can they be mitigated?
6. In what scenarios would spot instances be inappropriate? How can reliability be maintained?
7. How does workload scheduling help align cloud usage with business and cost goals?
10. Why is cultural resistance a major barrier to optimization, and how can it be addressed?
11. How does multi-cloud complexity impact cost allocation, and what tools can help?
12. How can cost optimization contribute to sustainability and environmental goals?

Multiple Choice Questions

1. Which of the following is the primary purpose of cost allocation in the Optimize phase?
    a. To reduce cloud provider bills through negotiation
    b. To assign cloud costs to specific teams, projects, or business units
    c. To migrate workloads to the cheapest cloud provider
    d. To automate software deployments

2. What is a key benefit of using tags in cloud cost management?
    a. They automatically shut down idle resources.
    b. They provide metadata to categorize and track spending by team, project, or environment.
    c. They reduce CPU utilization on virtual machines.
    d. They eliminate the need for reserved instances.
3. Which of the following best describes a chargeback model?
    a. Teams receive cost reports but are not financially responsible.
    b. Cloud costs are directly allocated to departments for budgeting and accountability.
    c. Costs are hidden from teams to avoid conflicts.
    d. Only the finance team manages all cloud spending.
4. What is the main risk of using spot instances?
    a. Higher long-term costs
    b. Limited availability in certain regions
    c. Risk of interruption when cloud provider needs capacity back
    d. Incompatibility with Linux workloads
5. Which organization saved $10 million annually by deleting unused S3 data?
    a. Netflix
    b. Spotify
    c. Dropbox
    d. Etsy
6. What is a best practice for overcoming inconsistent tagging?
    a. Allow teams to use their own naming conventions
    b. Disable tagging after initial setup
    c. Standardize naming conventions and automate enforcement using tools like AWS SCPs or Azure Policy
    d. Rely on manual audits only

7. Which of the following is a real-world benefit of rightsizing?
   a. Increased server redundancy
   b. Higher carbon emissions
   c. 25% cost reduction without performance loss (as seen in a healthcare startup)
   d. Elimination of the need for monitoring
8. What is a key challenge in multi-cloud environments?
   a. All cloud providers use the same pricing model
   b. Unified cost visibility and allocation are difficult due to siloed data
   c. Spot instances are not available on all platforms
   d. Reserved instances are interchangeable across providers
9. How can organizations balance cost savings and performance during optimization?
   a. Shut down all non-production environments
   b. Use monitoring tools to ensure performance thresholds are maintained
   c. Migrate all workloads to spot instances
   d. Avoid any changes to production systems
10. Which of the following supports both cost optimization and sustainability goals?
    a. Increasing server redundancy
    b. Running all workloads on premium instances
    c. Eliminating idle resources, which reduces energy use and CO_2 emissions
    d. Avoiding reserved instances

Answers

1. b
2. b
3. b
4. c
5. c
6. c
7. c
8. b
9. b
10. c

CHAPTER 5

Operate Phase: Visibility and Allocation

Introduction

Imagine signing up for a gym membership, working out religiously for a month, and finally hitting your fitness goals. But then life gets busy; you skip a week, then a month, and before you know it, you have lost all progress. The same thing happens with cloud cost management. Organizations often optimize their cloud spending, celebrate the savings, and then watch expenses creep back up as teams revert to old habits. Developers spin up untagged resources "just in case", budgets are ignored in the rush to meet deadlines, and unused assets pile up like forgotten gym equipment in a basement. This is the harsh reality for companies that treat FinOps as a one-time cleanup rather than daily discipline.

The Operate phase is where FinOps becomes a habit; it is the rhythm woven into the fabric of daily workflows. It is not enough to optimize costs once; you must nurture a culture where cost awareness is as routine as morning coffee. This phase ensures that cloud financial management is not a fleeting initiative but a sustained practice that evolves with your business.

Think of it as tending to a garden. The Inform phase is like planting the seeds (visibility), the Optimize phase resembles pruning and fertilizing (action), and the Operate phase is the consistent maintenance tasks like watering, weeding, and monitoring growth. Without this daily attention, even the most meticulously planned garden will wither. By the end of this chapter, you will master implementing automated governance and continuous monitoring to sustain cost optimization. You will also learn to embed FinOps into daily workflows and measure operational health through key metrics.

Structure

In this chapter, we will cover the following topics:

- Establishing Policies and Controls for Cost Management
- Reviewing Cloud Costs and Performance Metrics
- Create cross-functional feedback loops
- Maintain optimization gains through discipline
- Embed FinOps into daily workflows
- Measure operational health with key metrics

Establishing Policies and Controls for Cost Management

Cloud cost optimization is not a one-time project; it is an ongoing priority. This is where the **Operate phase** of FinOps comes in. After initial savings are achieved in the Inform and Optimize phases, the Operate phase ensures that progress is not lost and cloud usage remains efficient as the organization continues to scale. This phase is about embedding **long-term cost control mechanisms**—not just reacting to overages, but proactively preventing them. From setting guardrails to defining ownership, the Operate phase keeps cloud environments aligned with business goals.

The Operate phase is the glue that holds FinOps together. Here is why it is critical:

- **Prevents Regression: Stopping the Slide Back into Waste**

  Without sustained effort, teams slip into old habits. For instance, a SaaS company might optimize its databases one quarter, only to see costs rebound as engineers provision oversized instances for new features. The Operate phase combats this through:

  - **Automated Governance:** Tools such as AWS Service Control Policies (SCPs) block untagged resources.
  - **Routine Audits:** Monthly checks for zombie assets (such as idle servers and stale data).
  - **Embedded Accountability:** Teams own their costs, while making mindful spending their default behaviour.

Case Study: Automating Savings with Smart Scheduling at Monzo Bank

In the **Operate phase** of FinOps, automation becomes the backbone of sustained cost efficiency. It's not enough to perform one-time optimizations – organizations must build habits and systems that ensure resources continuously align with business needs. A strong example of this discipline in action comes from **Monzo Bank**[1], a cloud-native fintech company that embedded cost awareness directly into its engineering operations.

Background

Monzo Bank, a UK-based digital challenger bank founded in 2015, runs entirely on **Amazon Web Services (AWS)** to power its mobile banking platform. As customer demand grew and new features were rolled out, Monzo's engineering teams noticed that **non-production environments** – including development, testing, and staging – were frequently left running outside of business hours.

These idle environments generated thousands of dollars in unnecessary monthly costs, prompting Monzo to refine its operational practices as part of its broader **FinOps Operate framework**.

Challenge

By 2019, Monzo's AWS footprint had expanded significantly. Teams working across time zones often spun up temporary instances for testing or feature validation, but without a consistent mechanism for automated shutdowns, many of these instances remained active overnight or through weekends.

This inefficiency created a growing gap between infrastructure usage and business value – a classic FinOps problem where **optimization needed to evolve into automation**.

---

[1] This case study draws on Monzo's publicly documented engineering practices and cloud efficiency initiatives, particularly their approach to dynamic scaling and platform optimization. For reference, see:

- **Monzo Engineering Blog**: "Autoscaling Monzo: How we optimise our platform to be just the right size." Retrieved from https://monzo.com/blog/2020/10/19/autoscaling-monzo
- **Monzo Engineering Blog**: "Protecting our platform from spikes in usage by reducing load from the Monzo app." Retrieved from https://monzo.com/blog/2023/10/12/protecting-our-platform-from-spikes-in-usage-by-reducing-load-from-the-monzo
- **AWS Solutions Implementation**: Instance Scheduler on AWS https://aws.amazon.com/solutions/implementations/instance-scheduler-on-aws/

Approach Taken

To address this, Monzo's **Platform Engineering** team extended their existing autoscaling and monitoring systems to include **Automated Scheduling Policies** using **AWS Instance Scheduler**, **Lambda functions**, and **internal orchestration scripts**.

These were configured to:

- Automatically shut down **non-production EC2 instances and RDS databases** after 8:00 PM UTC.
- Restart environments each morning before development resumes.
- Send real-time **Slack notifications** to development teams before shutdown, offering opt-out flexibility for active workloads.

This blend of automation and communication allowed Monzo to maintain agility while minimizing waste – embedding FinOps discipline into their daily workflows.

Impact

Within 3 months of implementation, Monzo achieved measurable results:

- 30% reduction in non-production compute hours.
- Over $10,000 in monthly AWS savings.
- Improved developer accountability through clear visibility into resource usage.

The initiative reinforced Monzo's FinOps maturity, ensuring that **cost optimization became an ongoing operational rhythm**, not a one-time cleanup.

Lessons Learned

- Automating shutdowns of idle resources is one of the quickest and most sustainable FinOps wins.
- Balancing automation with developer flexibility prevents resistance and fosters adoption.
- Continuous review of automation policies ensures that savings persist as systems evolve.

Case Study: TRC Healthcare Cloud Cost Optimization Fuels Innovation in Healthcare

TRC Healthcare [2], a leading provider of clinical knowledge solutions for healthcare professionals, faced rising AWS costs as its digital health platforms expanded to meet increased demand. During the **Operate phase**, the organization's IT and finance teams launched a **FinOps-driven initiative** to enhance visibility, reduce inefficiencies, and redirect savings toward innovation.

Optimization Actions

1. Conducted a detailed analysis of compute and database workloads to identify steady-state usage and forecast capacity needs.
2. Adopted a hybrid cost-optimization model using **1-year Reserved Instances (RIs)** and **AWS Savings Plans** to reduce reliance on On-Demand pricing.
3. Implemented continuous monitoring and anomaly detection using **nOps**, providing real-time insights into cost drivers and enabling proactive governance.
4. Applied rightsizing and automated scheduling for nonproduction environments to further eliminate waste and improve utilization.

Outcomes and Reinvestment

Through these actions, TRC Healthcare achieved **significant AWS cost reductions** while maintaining scalability and performance. Rather than treating the savings purely as cost-cutting, leadership reinvested part of the recovered budget into developing an **AI-powered patient engagement portal**.

This innovation leverages **machine learning** to deliver features such as real-time symptom triage, medication reminders, and automated follow-ups—enhancing both patient satisfaction and clinician efficiency.

Operate Phase Insight

The TRC Healthcare example illustrates that the **Operate phase** of the cloud journey is not only about managing and optimizing spend—it's a strategic opportunity to **transform operational efficiency into innovation and competitive advantage**.

---

[2] Based on the verified case study: "*TRC Healthcare Leverages nOps for Enhanced AWS Cost Optimization and Scalability.*"

Available at: https://www.nops.io/casestudies/trc-healthcare-leverages-nops-for-enhanced-aws-cost-optimization-and-scalability/

The Hidden Cost of Neglecting the Operate Phase

Skipping the Operate phase in cloud financial management is like ignoring your cloud environment's health checks and usage reports. Everything might seem fine at first, but over time, unmanaged resources, lack of monitoring, and outdated configurations can lead to budget overruns, performance degradation, and missed optimization opportunities. Just because it is working now does not mean it is running efficiently. For instance:

- A retail company saved $100,000 during Black Friday by optimizing resources but saw costs double six months later due to unmonitored scaling.
- An e-commerce team's failure to update tags led to $25,000 wasted monthly on orphaned storage buckets.

The Operate Phase in Action: Capital One's Cultural Shift

Capital One[3] did not just optimize cloud costs—they made FinOps a daily ritual. When Capital One migrated to the cloud, the company recognized that financial accountability needed to evolve alongside technical agility. Rather than treating cost optimization as an occasional task, Capital One embedded FinOps into its culture, turning cost awareness into a daily engineering habit that drives both efficiency and innovation.

Key Practices:

- **Governance Policies**: Mandatory tagging for every resource, enforced via automation.
- **Automated Cleanup**: Scripts delete unused instances after 7 days.
- **Cross-Team Rituals**: Weekly "Cost Standups" where engineers and finance teams review spending together.

Results:

- 25% reduction in cloud costs within a year
- Zero zombie assets due to proactive monitoring
- Faster product launches because teams could self-serve resources within budget guardrails

[3] Details on Capital One's FinOps and cloud cost management practices are drawn from: *Capital One Tech Blog – "Best Practices: Optimize Cloud Spend with FinOps."* Available at: https://www.capitalone.com/tech/cloud/cloud-cost-management/

Completing the FinOps Lifecycle Through the Operate Phase

The Operate phase closes the loop of the FinOps lifecycle (Inform → Optimize → Operate → Repeat). It ensures that:

- Visibility is maintained through updated dashboards and alerts.
- Optimization is ongoing with regular rightsizing and reserved instance reviews.
- Accountability is reinforced through chargeback models and team KPIs.

The FinOps Flywheel consists of **Visibility**, which leads to **Action** and **Culture**, which both result in **Continuous Improvement**.

Case Study: Spotify's Daily FinOps Rituals

Company: Spotify

Challenge: As cloud usage scaled rapidly, Spotify faced rising infrastructure costs and limited cost visibility for engineering teams. This threatened budget control while risking slower delivery if engineers were forced into manual cost reviews.

Solution:

- **Automated Cost Alerts:** Real-time Slack notifications warn engineers when resource usage exceeds predefined budget thresholds.
- **Gamified Savings:** Teams compete to reduce costs, with top performers celebrated in internal newsletters, fostering a healthy, fun sense of competition.
- **FinOps in DevOps:** Cost reviews are now built into every sprint retrospective, ensuring that cost awareness becomes part of the regular engineering rhythm, rather than an afterthought.

Result: Spotify achieved a **15% year-over-year cloud cost reduction** and built a culture where engineers proactively optimize resources without sacrificing innovation speed[4].

Key Lessons and Takeaways

- **Embed FinOps into daily engineering practices** to ensure cost awareness is continuous, and a not occasional occurrence

[4] McKinsey & Company – *Everything is better as code: Using FinOps to manage cloud costs.* Retrieved from https://www.mckinsey.com/capabilities/mckinsey-digital/our-insights/everything-is-better-as-code-using-finops-to-manage-cloud-costs

- **Gamification encourages participation** and drives team engagement in cost-reduction initiatives
- **Automation reduces overhead and enables** faster and more informed decision-making

The Human Side of the Operate Phase

FinOps truly comes alive during the Operate phase. It is not because of dashboards or policies, but because of the people who embrace it in their daily routines.

Engineers begin to think more intentionally. Before provisioning a large instance, they pause and consider whether it is truly necessary. Cost awareness becomes part of their development process, instead of a separate concern handed down later.

Finance teams, in turn, start to build real trust in the engineering teams. They no longer feel the need to micromanage or second-guess cloud decisions. Instead, they see engineers making responsible choices, staying within budgets, and collaborating openly when forecasts shift.

The leadership also begins to initiate a shift in its perspective. FinOps is no longer seen as a cost-cutting exercise. It becomes a strategic capability and a way to innovate smarter, scale responsibly, and make data-driven decisions that support long-term goals.

When FinOps becomes a shared mindset rather than just a framework, the Operate phase becomes less about control and more about continuous improvement, trust, and alignment across the organization.

Case Study: Embedding Cost Awareness

Engineering teams began incorporating **cloud cost estimates**[5] into every project proposal, ensuring that financial considerations were embedded early in the design and planning process. This alignment between technical decisions and business objectives fostered **stronger collaboration between engineering and finance**, improved budget forecasting, and encouraged more thoughtful use of cloud resources.

---

[5] This approach reflects recommendations from Google Cloud's "*Foster a Culture of Cost Awareness*" framework, which encourages including cost estimates in architecture planning to align financial and technical goals.

Available at: https://cloud.google.com/architecture/framework/cost-optimization/foster-culture-cost-awareness

Over time, this practice evolved into a **cultural norm**. Teams became proactive about **rightsizing workloads**, avoiding unnecessary services, and discussing potential budget impacts before deployment. Financial accountability was no longer seen as a constraint–it became a **shared responsibility** that enhanced delivery speed and fueled innovation.

A similar approach was adopted by Atlassian, where engineering teams are empowered to manage their own cloud budgets through transparent cost metrics and decentralized accountability. Atlassian implemented real-time dashboards and unit cost tracking, enabling teams to make informed decisions that align cloud usage with both product performance and financial targets.[6]

Looking Ahead

The Operate phase is not about rigidity, but about resilience. As we dive deeper, we will unpack tools, techniques, and cultural strategies to keep your cloud costs in check while fueling growth.

Reviewing Cloud Costs and Performance Metrics

Governance plays a critical role in shaping and sustaining cloud cost performance. It establishes the **guardrails and measurement standards** that help organizations monitor, manage, and improve cloud spending in alignment with strategic goals. Effective cloud governance is built upon several core principles that ensure cost management is consistent, scalable, and aligned with business objectives. These foundational tenets include:

- **Establishes Cost Performance Benchmarks**

  Governance defines what "good" looks like. This might be setting cost KPIs (for example cost per service and unit cost per feature) and enabling teams to track progress consistently.

- **Enforces Financial Accountability**: By setting budgets, tagging policies, and access controls, governance ensures that teams are accountable for their cloud usage and spending.

[6] *FinOps Foundation – Atlassian FinOps Case Study*. This case study describes how Atlassian successfully embedded FinOps practices into engineering workflows by decentralizing cloud budget ownership and implementing real-time cost visibility. Available at: https://www.finops.org/community/stories/atlassian-finops/

- **Aligns Spending with Business Priorities**: Governance frameworks tie cloud investments to outcomes, such as supporting product launches, optimizing operations, or achieving sustainability targets.
- **Enables Data-Driven Decisions**: Standardized cost metrics and dashboards provide leaders with the visibility needed to make informed trade-offs between performance, cost, and innovation.
- **Encourages Cross-Functional Collaboration**: Governance fosters collaboration across finance, engineering, and operations by creating a shared language and process around cloud cost performance.

Key Governance Policies

Effective governance requires concrete policies that automate enforcement and establish clear accountability. These key policies form the foundation of sustainable cloud cost management:

- **Mandatory Tagging:** Tags are metadata labels that categorize resources by team, project, or environment. For example:
    - A retail company tags resources by campaign (example, "Holiday 2023")
    - A healthcare organization tags resources by department (example, "Patient Analytics")
- **Real-World Example – Spotify:** After discovering $2 million wasted annually on unused Kubernetes clusters, Spotify enforced a tagging policy requiring labels such as "Team: Recommendations" or "Environment: QA." This enabled them to track costs precisely and attribute accountability.
- **Budget Thresholds:** Setting spending limits for departments or projects prevents surprises. For instance:
    - A SaaS provider allocates $50,000 monthly to its marketing team for cloud campaigns
    - A gaming company sets thresholds for compute costs tied to user growth projections
- **Approval Workflows:** Restricting high-cost actions (for example, launching 100+ instances) leads to oversight. Tools such as AWS Service Catalog or Azure Blueprints standardize approvals.

Best Practices for Effective Governance

- **Automate Enforcement:** Manual governance is error-prone and time-consuming. Use tools such as AWS Service Control Policies (SCPs) or Azure Policy to block non-compliant actions automatically.

  - **Example**: A fintech company uses SCPs to prevent untagged resources from being deployed, reducing waste by 18%
- **Start Small, Scale Gradually:** Pilot policies with one team or project to refine processes before expanding.
  - **Case Study**: A media startup tested mandatory tagging with its QA team, achieving 95% compliance in two weeks. They then rolled it out company-wide
- **Document Rules in a "Cloud Governance Handbook":** Create a shared playbook outlining tagging standards, budget limits, and approval processes.
  - **Tip**: Include screenshots of tools and workflows to make guidelines actionable
- **Leverage Role-Based Access Control (RBAC):** Restrict permissions to prevent accidental overspending. For example, only senior engineers can approve large instance deployments.

Visualizing Governance in Action

Here is a simplified workflow diagram to illustrate how governance policies work:

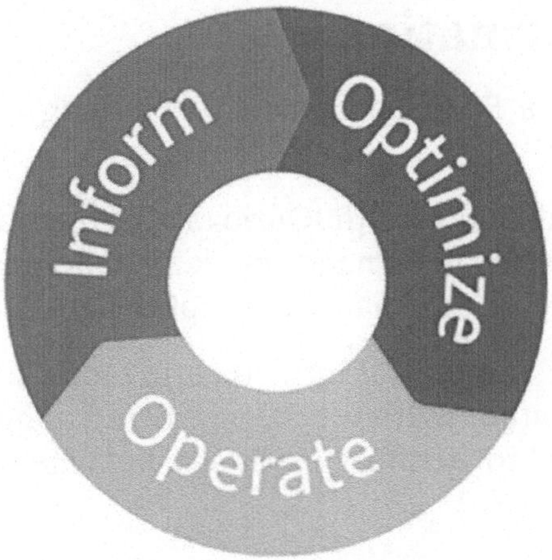

Figure 5.1: *Finops phases*

Tools to Support Governance

To maintain consistent standards and enforce compliance across cloud environments, organizations rely on specialized governance tools like the ones mentioned here:

- **AWS Config:** Monitors compliance with tagging and configuration rules
- **Azure Policy:** Enforces policies across multi-cloud environments

- **Custom Scripts:** Automate cleanup of untagged resources using Python or Terraform

The Human Side of Governance

Governance is not about micromanaging–it is about empowering teams to innovate responsibly. Successful governance relies on a set of human-centric principles that ensure policies are adopted effectively, rather than being perceived as restrictive mandates. These foundational principles include:

- **Collaboration Over Control:** Involve teams in policy creation. For example, ask developers what tagging structure works best for them
- **Education First:** Train teams on why policies matter. A workshop explaining how tagging prevents budget overruns can turn skeptics into advocates

The FinOps Foundation framework emphasizes that the fundamental goal of governance is to "enable informed, timely, and cost-effective decision making," establishing guardrails that empower teams to innovate within safe financial boundaries rather than imposing restrictive controls.[71]

Real-World Impact: Ouribank's Governance and FinOps Transformation

Company: Ouribank [8] – a Brazilian fintech specializing in currency exchange and financial services.

Overview: Facing rapid digital growth, Ouribank partnered with a FinOps team and e-Core to create a centralized governance model that delivered full visibility into AWS spend and enabled proactive, automated cost optimization.

Challenge: In 2023, the company's infrastructure costs surged by over 140% as cloud adoption accelerated. Without standardized tagging or centralized cost visibility, teams struggled to attribute expenses, manage reservations, and forecast budgets effectively.

Solution:

- **Centralized Cost Visibility:** Implemented a unified platform to track all AWS spending by team, product, and service.

---

[7] "Principles," *FinOps Foundation*, https://www.finops.org/framework/principles/.

[8] *"How Ouribank achieved 60% cloud savings with a FinOps strategy and AWS expertise,"* e-Core Case Study, accessed 2025. □ https://www.e-core.com/na-en/case-study/finops-aws-ouribank-cloud-savings

- **Automated Governance:** Introduced tagging standards, automated resource scheduling, and storage optimization policies.
- **Empowered Engineering:** Equipped engineers with real-time cost insights and ownership of their budgets, promoting accountability and faster decision-making.

Results:

- **60% reduction** in overall cloud costs.
- **70% Savings Plans coverage** across eligible workloads.
- **94% tagging compliance**, enabling precise cost attribution.
- Enhanced operational efficiency and improved financial predictability across teams.

Key Lessons: Centralizing cost and usage data builds the foundation for governance. Empowering engineers with transparent cost data fosters accountability, while automation ensures savings are sustained over time.

Real-World Impact: Adobe's Cost Governance Overhaul

Company: Adobe[9], creators of the Adobe Experience Platform and other cloud-driven services.

Overview: As Adobe's Experience Platform growth exploded, so did its cloud costs. To maintain agility while keeping spend under control, Adobe implemented a cost governance program that embedded financial awareness into engineering operations, improved visibility across infrastructure, and automated cost optimization.

Challenge: Growth of services and data pipelines led to overspending. Categories like storage, compute, network transit, and abandoned resources (snapshots, block storage) were major contributors to waste. Lack of consistent cost reporting and automated tools made it difficult to spot inefficiencies early.

Solution:

- **Detailed cost breakdowns** by region, service, and usage to identify where overspend was occurring.
- **Focused optimization**: VM rightsizing, removing abandoned/dormant resources, reducing overprovisioned storage.

---

[9] "*Adobe Experience Platform Pipeline Cost Management: A Case Study*," Adobe Tech Blog, April 30, 2020. https://blog.developer.adobe.com/adobe-experience-platform-pipeline-cost-management-a-case-study-2c3f74841a2e blog.developer.adobe.com

- Built dashboards and reporting tools to enable cost governance as a continuous practice, not a one-time fix.

Results:

- Adobe significantly reduced excessive spending in key categories (storage and compute) where most waste was found.
- Better visibility and ongoing cost governance prevented overprovisioning and unused resource accumulation.
- Project planning and infrastructure decisions began to incorporate cost implications as a standard part of design and operations.

Key Lessons and Takeaways:

- Deep visibility into spend (service, region, usage) unlocks the ability to find real optimization opportunities.
- Using reporting tools and dashboards helps make financial accountability part of engineering's workflow.
- Automating cleanup, rightsizing, and oversight maintains cost discipline while enabling growth.

Strategic Benefits of Strong Governance

Strong governance creates benefits beyond cost savings which are as follows:

- **Improved Collaboration**: Finance and engineering teams speak the same language
- **Faster Innovation**: Teams know their boundaries and can act autonomously within them
- **Sustainability Wins**: Reduced waste aligns with ESG goals

Governance as a Foundation

Governance policies are the bedrock of the Operate phase. They ensure that cost awareness becomes a habit and not a hurdle.

As Erik Peterson, CTO at CloudZero, has noted, engineering teams need "clear cost guardrails and goals" early in development – otherwise they end up spending far more time in cost-cutting meetings later. This principle reflects a common FinOps truth: without financial visibility, even skilled engineers can lose sight of the bigger picture.

Source: Erik Peterson, "Million-Dollar Lines of Code: Embracing Shift-Left FinOps and Engineering-Led Cloud Optimization," CloudZero Blog, 2024.

https://tfsy.io/million-dollar-lines-of-code-embracing-shift-left-finops-and-engineering-led-cloud-optimization

By embedding governance into daily workflows, organizations can sustain FinOps' success and fuel growth for themselves.

The Importance of Routine Reviews: Staying Ahead in Cloud Management

Think of routine cloud cost reviews as your organization's fitness tracker for maintaining cloud health. Just like you'd monitor your heart rate or step count to stay in shape, keeping an eye on cloud metrics ensures your spending remains efficient and aligned with business goals. Weekly or monthly reviews are the backbone of the **"Operate"** phase in cloud management. They keep teams aligned, budgets on track, and resources optimized. Without them, even the most well-thought-out FinOps strategies can quickly fall apart.

Key Metrics that Drive Action

To make cloud cost data truly actionable, organizations must track metrics that tie spending directly to business value, turning abstract numbers into decisions that drive efficiency and growth. Some of these metrics are as follows:

- **Cost Per Unit:** This metric connects spending to tangible business outcomes. For example:
  - A retail company might track the cost per online transaction to evaluate cloud efficiency
  - A SaaS provider could calculate the cloud expenses tied to supporting each customer

  Example: Etsy conducts quarterly sustainability reviews, identifying idle resources that contributed to a 15% reduction in CO_2 emissions by cutting energy waste. By linking cost data to environmental impact, they turned savings into a win for sustainability.

- **Utilization Rates:** Low utilization rates often signal wasted resources.

  Example: A streaming service noticed its video transcoding servers were running at just 30% capacity. After rightsizing, they cut costs by 20% without affecting performance.

- **ROI of Cloud Investments:** Are your cloud resources driving revenue or improving customer satisfaction?

Example: A fintech startup measured the ROI of its AI-driven fraud detection system, proving it justified the premium compute costs.

Tools to Enhance Review and Reporting

The right tools can transform cloud cost reviews from static reports into dynamic, data-driven insights that uncover hidden inefficiencies and guide smarter decisions. Some of the tools are:

- **AWS Cost Explorer:** Breaks down costs by service, region, or tag. For instance, a logistics company used it to uncover $50,000 wasted monthly on unused storage.
- **Custom Dashboards (like Tableau and Grafana):** Visualize trends and correlations. A gaming company built a dashboard showing the cost per active user, helping prioritize optimizations
- **Third-Party Platforms (such as CloudHealth and Apptio):** Offer multi-cloud insights. A global retailer, **Loblaw Companies Limited**[1] used CloudHealth to track spending across AWS and Azure, saving **$768,000** within seven months

Real-World Example: Loblaw's CloudHealth Journey

Canada's largest food and pharmacy retailer, **Loblaw Companies Limited**[10], used **VMware CloudHealth** to gain financial visibility across its AWS and Azure environments. Before adoption, siloed teams struggled to understand which workloads were driving costs or how to optimize them effectively.

By centralizing cost monitoring and applying automated policies to flag idle resources, Loblaw improved governance, aligned IT and finance, and achieved **over $768,000 in savings within seven months**. The company transformed cloud cost management from a reactive exercise into a proactive, data-driven discipline – demonstrating how tools like **CloudHealth** and **Apptio** can unify technical and financial accountability across complex, multi-cloud landscapes.

---

[10] "*Loblaw Companies Limited: Improving Financial Visibility and Cloud Governance with VMware CloudHealth*," VMware Case Study, 2021.
https://assets.contentstack.io/v3/assets/blt9e072702140c498e/blt1654d8d1d73514fc/603d5c611a42e25ce54e60ff/Loblaw_CloudHealth_Case_Study.pdf

Best Practices for Impactful Reviews

For cloud cost reviews to create real impact, the insights must be packaged for the right audience, ensuring each stakeholder receives information that matches their priorities and decision-making need. Some of the best practices are to:

- **Tailor Reports as per Your Audience's Requirements**
  - **Executives**: Provide high-level summaries with strategic implications
  - **Engineers**: Share granular data on resource usage and optimization opportunities
  - **Finance Teams**: Focus on budget adherence and forecast accuracy

  Example: A healthcare company created a "CFO Dashboard" highlighting quarterly savings and a "DevOps Dashboard" pinpointing underutilized clusters.

- **Pair Cost with Performance Metrics:** Track latency, uptime, or error rates alongside costs

  Example: A SaaS provider noticed a spike in latency linked to overprovisioned databases. Rightsizing improved performance and saved $35,000 monthly.

- **Schedule Reviews Consistently**
  - Weekly 15-minute stand-ups for engineering teams
  - Monthly deep dives with finance and leadership

  Case Study: Adobe's monthly "Cost Sync-Ups" reduced cloud waste by 18% by aligning technical decisions with financial goals.

- **Use Benchmarks for Context**

  Compare your metrics to industry standards.

  Example: A media company realized its storage costs were 30% higher than peers, prompting lifecycle management improvements.

- **Turning Data into Actionable Insights:** Reviews are not just about numbers, but about crafting a story. Transforming raw data into compelling narratives fosters collaboration, accountability, and innovation. When done right, organizations can create a culture where cost awareness becomes second nature.

Bridging Teams Through Collaborative Analysis

One of the most powerful aspects of reviews is their ability to unite teams. Finance and engineering often operate in silos, but collaborative analysis breaks down these barriers.

Here is an example that illustrates the impact of comprehensive reviews:

A retail company held a joint review session between finance and engineering teams. Together, they identified $20,000 wasted on zombie assets like idle servers and unused storage buckets forgotten over time. Within hours, engineers decommissioned these resources, turning abstract numbers into immediate savings.

This kind of collaboration not only saves money but also builds trust. When finance teams see engineers taking ownership of costs and engineers understand the financial implications of their decisions, alignment improves across the board.

Best Practices for Collaborative Reviews

- Invite cross-functional teams to ensure that both finance and technical stakeholders are present
- Focus on solutions rather than assigning blame
- Use visuals such as dashboards and charts to make complex data easier to digest

Celebrating Progress: Reinforcing Positive Behaviors

Highlighting wins, whether they are big or small, is crucial for maintaining momentum. Celebrating progress motivates teams to continue optimizing and reinforces the value of FinOps practices.

Case Study: An e-commerce company celebrated a 30% cost reduction in QA environments during a team meeting. The achievement was shared in the company newsletter, and the engineering team was recognized for it by the leadership. This acknowledgment boosted morale and inspired other teams to adopt similar practices, creating a ripple effect of optimization efforts.

Ways to Celebrate Wins:

- Public recognition in meetings, newsletters, or platforms such as Slack
- Tie savings to broader business goals, such as funding new projects
- Gamify optimization by creating friendly competitions between teams

While automated alerts and dashboards provide essential data, the true engine of sustainable cost optimization is human conversation. As David May[111], a FinOps leader,

[11] David May, "Scaling FinOps Collaboration in Complex Organizations: A Data-Driven, Human-Centered Approach," *Medium*, 2023, https://medium.com/@david_22825/scaling-finops-collaboration-in-complex-organizations-a-data-driven-human-centered-approach-e0ee5a70858d.

articulates in his analysis of scaling collaboration, "Automated messages don't build trust. Face-to-face or camera-to-camera conversations are what move the needle."[1]

This insight underscores why structured review sessions are a cornerstone of the Operate phase. The goal of these reviews is to transform raw financial data into a compelling narrative that connects cloud spending directly to business outcomes. This shift in framing turns accountability from a punitive exercise into a motivational one.

For instance, instead of a report stating, "*The engineering team saved $50,000 this quarter*," a more powerful narrative would be:

"By rightsizing our database clusters, the platform team saved $50,000—funding that has been reallocated to develop two new features projected to help us acquire 10,000 new customers."

This approach demonstrates a fundamental principle of the Operate phase: numbers inform, but stories inspire. It is in these collaborative forums, where data meets dialogue, that FinOps evolves from a mechanical cost-control function into a genuine catalyst for strategic innovation and cross-functional alignment.

Common Pitfalls and Solutions

- **Analysis Paralysis**

  Too much data overwhelms teams.

  Solution: Focus on 3-5 key metrics per review

- **Ignoring Trends**

  A one-time review will not sustain savings.

  Solution: Track metrics over time. (Example: "Compute costs have risen 10% monthly; why is it happening?")

- **Siloed Reviews**

  Finance and engineering review data separately.

  Solution: Host cross-functional meetings to align perspectives

The Strategic Value of Routine Assessments

When done right, reviews create benefits beyond cost savings:

- **Strategic Alignment**: Cloud spending funds innovation, not waste
- **Trust-Building**: Finance and engineering collaborate instead of clash
- **Sustainability**: Reduced energy consumption supports ESG goals

Automation for Sustainable Efficiency

Automation reduces manual effort and prevents human error. Examples include:

- Shut down scripts to turn off idle development environments at night
- Auto-scaling to adjust resources dynamically based on demand
- Zombie hunter tools to scan for and delete unused storage or instances

Case Study: Slack's Scaled Resilience and Cost Efficiency

Company: Slack – a widely used collaboration and messaging platform.

Challenge: As Slack's user base and internal services grew, the engineering team needed to ensure reliable performance during unpredictable peaks, without overspending on idle infrastructure.

Solution (types):

- **Auto-Scaling (Dynamic Provisioning):** Slack adopted **Karpenter** on AWS to manage node provisioning and termination dynamically, scaling compute capacity to match real-time demand.[1]
- **Cluster Consolidation/Bin-Packing:** By consolidating workloads into fewer nodes, Slack reduced underutilization and minimized waste.
- **(Type-aware) Predictive Scaling:** While the blog doesn't explicitly mention predictive models, Slack's use of Karpenter's optimizations implies they anticipate scaling needs ahead of sudden load surges.
- **Governance and Policy Enforcement:** Slack enforces autoscaling policies and uses cost-conscious scheduling to keep resource usage efficient.

Results: Slack achieved improved cost efficiency and operational flexibility by aligning resource allocation to workload demand, reducing unnecessary idle capacity.[12]

Expert Insight: "*Automation turns cost optimization from a project into a practice*," says Mark Thompson, Cloud Economist.

---

[12] "*How Slack adopted Karpenter to increase operational and cost efficiency*," AWS Blog (2024) https://aws.amazon.com/blogs/containers/how-slack-adopted-karpenter-to-increase-operational-and-cost-efficiency/

Building a Culture of Continuous Improvement

FinOps thrives when teams take ownership of their spending. Some of these strategies include:

- **Celebrating Wins**: Recognize teams that cut costs without harming performance
- **Educating Regularly**: Host workshops on cost-saving techniques such as spot instances
- **Encouraging Open Dialogue**: Finance and engineering teams review budgets and forecasts together

Real-World Example – Adobe: The FinOps team at Adobe holds monthly "Cost Clinics" where engineers present optimization wins, which fosters friendly competition and accountability.

Advanced Techniques: Chargeback and Showback Models:

- **Chargeback**: Directly bill teams for their cloud usage (such as, internal "cloud credits")
- **Showback**: Share cost reports without financial penalties to encourage mindfulness

Example – Dropbox: Dropbox uses a showback model to highlight team spending, reducing waste by 20% without creating friction.

Here are some tips that might help in achieving similar results:

- Start with a show back to build trust
- Use tools such as Apptio or Cloudability for chargeback reporting

Overcoming Common Challenges

Some of the topmost challenges in the Operate phase include tool sprawl, changing usage patterns, and cultural silos. Solutions involve consolidating tools, using flexible savings plans, and hosting regular cross-department reviews.

Conclusion

Operate phase, adopting FinOps is a Daily Discipline.

The Operate phase ensures FinOps isn't not a flash-in-the-pan initiative but a daily discipline. By automating processes, enforcing policies, and nurturing collaboration, organizations can sustain cost efficiency while fueling innovation.

Call to Action: "Start small–automate one task, enforce one policy, celebrate one win. Then repeat. That's is how FinOps becomes a way of life."

The next chapter is on cloud cost management tools.

Key Terms

- **Cloud Governance**: The framework of policies, processes, and tools that ensure cloud usage aligns with business objectives, compliance standards, and cost efficiency.
- **FinOps**: A financial operations framework that brings together engineering, finance, and business teams to manage cloud spending effectively.
- **Resource Tagging**: Applying metadata labels to cloud resources for tracking, accountability, and cost allocation.
- **Budget Alerts**: Automated notifications triggered when cloud spending approaches predefined limits.
- **Approval Gates**: Governance checkpoints requiring review before high-cost or sensitive cloud resources are deployed.
- **Infrastructure-as-Code (IaC)**: The practice of managing and provisioning computing infrastructure through machine-readable definition files (for example, Terraform, AWS CloudFormation).
- **Lifecycle Policies**: Automated rules for moving or archiving unused data to optimize storage costs.

Points to Remember

- Cloud governance is not just about cutting costs, but about ensuring every dollar spent drives measurable business value.
- Tagging and budget controls improve transparency and help identify cost anomalies early.
- Approval workflows protect budgets without slowing down innovation if they are automated and clearly documented.
- Regular review meetings across engineering, finance, and leadership teams ensure accountability and proactive decision-making.
- Using tools such as **AWS Cost Explorer**, **Azure Policy**, and **Terraform** helps enforce governance at scale.

Questions

1. What are the main goals of cloud governance in an enterprise environment?
2. Explain how resource tagging can improve cost accountability.

3. How can milestone-based budgets help align technical and business objectives?
4. Why is automation important in approval workflows?
5. Give an example of a lifecycle policy and explain its cost benefits.

Multiple Choice Questions

1. Which of the following best describes FinOps?
    a. A cloud provider's native monitoring tool
    b. A financial framework for optimizing cloud costs
    c. A type of virtual machine for budget tracking
    d. An AI-powered cost prediction engine
2. Which governance control ensures resources have identifiable ownership?
    a. Budget Alerts
    b. Lifecycle Policies
    c. Resource Tagging
    d. Serverless Automation
3. What is the main purpose of approval gates?
    a. To block all high-cost requests
    b. To ensure expensive deployments are justified
    c. To automate serverless workloads
    d. To enforce encryption
4. Which tool can enforce multi-cloud governance policies?
    a. AWS Cost Explorer
    b. Azure Policy
    c. AWS Lambda
    d. Grafana

5. Lifecycle policies in AWS S3 are used to:
    a. Restrict access to buckets
    b. Archive or delete unused data automatically
    c. Track cost allocation by tags
    d. Send budget alerts

Answers

1. b
2. c
3. b
4. b
5. b

CHAPTER 6
Mastering Cloud Cost Management with FinOps Tools

Introduction

Cloud computing has transformed how businesses operate, offering unmatched scalability, flexibility, and innovation. Companies can now deploy applications faster, scale resources on demand, and avoid hefty upfront infrastructure costs. This shift has enabled organizations to focus on innovation rather than managing physical servers or data centers. However, the pay-as-you-go pricing model, while being flexible, can spiral out of control if not managed effectively.

The dynamic nature of cloud services often leads to inefficiencies like accumulation of unused resources, increase in costs due to overprovisioned instances, and misconfigurations that go unnoticed until they result in unexpected expenses. This underscores the need for disciplined cost management practices. Without proper oversight, cloud spending can quickly exceed budgets, negating the financial benefits that initially attracted organizations to the cloud.

By the end of this chapter, the reader will have a clear roadmap for implementing cloud cost management practices tailored to your organization's needs. Let's dive into the details.

Structure

In this chapter, we will cover the following topics:

- Overview of cloud cost management tools
- Setting up dashboards for visibility
- Integrating cost tools with third party platforms

The Growing Challenge of Cloud Cost Management

Despite the cost-saving potential of cloud services, many organizations struggle to keep their spending in check. Some of the common pain points include:

Lack of Visibility

Tracking expenses across multiple services, accounts, and teams is a major hurdle. Cloud providers offer dozens of services with complex pricing models (example per-second compute, data transfer fees, API call costs). Without centralized monitoring and consistent tagging, it is nearly impossible to understand who is spending, on what, and why.

For example, an organization might have hundreds of virtual machines (VMs) running across AWS, Azure, and GCP, but without proper tagging by team, project, or environment, identifying underutilized or orphaned resources becomes a manual, error-prone process.

✅ **FinOps Tip:** Implement mandatory tagging policies at the account level using tools like AWS Service Control Policies (SCPs) or Azure Policy. Require tags such as `Owner`, `Project`, `Environment`, and `CostCenter` before resources can be provisioned.

💡 **Watch Out:** Do not treat tagging as a one-time initiative. Teams often start strong but fall out of compliance over time. Automate enforcement; if tagging is not enforced, it will not be followed.

📘 **Exam Note:** The FinOps Certification exam frequently tests on the importance of resource tagging for cost allocation and chargeback/showback models. Know the difference between the two and how tagging enables both.

Unexpected Costs

Misconfigurations and forgotten resources are silent budget killers. A developer might spin up a high-performance database for a short-term test and forget to delete it. Or an autoscaling group might scale out during a traffic spike but fail to scale back in, leading to sustained overprovisioning.

These "zombie assets" (example unattached disks, idle load balancers, stale snapshots) can accumulate silently, costing thousands per month. According to McKinsey, ~28% of cloud spending is reported as waste due to such inefficiencies.

✅ **FinOps Tip:** Use automated cleanup policies to remove or shut down idle resources. For example, configure AWS Instance Scheduler or Azure Automation to power down non-production environments after business hours

💡 **Watch Out:** Assuming all cost spikes are wasteful. Some overages are legitimate (example product launches, traffic surges). Always pair cost data with performance and business context before taking action

📘 **Exam Note:** You will most likely encounter questions about identifying and eliminating zombie assets and the role of automated lifecycle policies. Be familiar with tools like AWS Config, Cloud Custodian, and Stacklet to detect idle resources

Multi-Cloud Complexity

Managing costs across AWS, Azure, and GCP introduces inconsistency in pricing models, tooling, and terminology. For example:

- AWS uses Savings Plans and Reserved Instances
- Azure offers Reserved VM Instances and Azure Hybrid Benefit
- GCP has Committed Use Discounts and Sustained Use Discounts

Without a unified cost management strategy, teams struggle to compare spend, enforce policies, or optimize consistently across platforms.

✅ **FinOps Tip:** Use multi-cloud cost management platforms like CloudHealth, Apptio, or Stacklet to gain a single pane of glass across providers. Standardize tagging and governance policies wherever possible

💡 **Watch Out:** Believing that multi-cloud = cost savings. In reality, without strong governance, multi-cloud often increases complexity and waste. Optimize first, then diversify

📘 **Exam Note:** The exam often includes scenarios involving multi-cloud cost allocation and comparing discount models. Know the differences between Savings Plans (AWS), Committed Use Discounts (GCP), and Reserved Instances (Azure)

Overview of Cloud Cost Management Tools

In this chapter, we will explore essential FinOps tools from leading cloud providers like AWS, Azure, and Google Cloud, as well as third-party platforms that offer advanced capabilities. These tools empower organizations to monitor, analyze, and optimize their cloud spending effectively.

Additionally, we will cover advanced strategies such as rightsizing resources, leveraging reserved instances, and implementing tagging best practices. Real-world examples and case studies will illustrate how organizations have successfully reduced their cloud costs by applying these techniques. By the end of this chapter, you will be equipped with actionable insights and practical steps to take control of your cloud spending.

Native Cloud Cost Management Tools

Native cloud cost management tools are built-in services provided by cloud platforms to help organizations monitor, analyze, and optimize their spending without relying on third-party solutions. They offer **real-time cost visibility**, **granular usage tracking**, and **forecasting capabilities** tailored to each platform's ecosystem.

AWS Cost Explorer

AWS Cost Explorer[1] is a powerful visualization tool designed to provide insights into your AWS spending patterns. It allows users to analyze historical data, forecast future costs, and identify anomalies.

Key Features:

- **Custom Reports:** Filter data by service, region, tags, or usage type. For example, you can create a report that shows EC2 costs broken down by instance type and region
- **Forecasting:** Predict future costs based on historical trends. This feature helps organizations plan budgets and avoid unexpected surprises
- **Anomaly Detection:** Identify unusual spikes in spending before they become major issues. For instance, if a team accidentally deploys a large number of high-performance instances, Cost Explorer will flag the anomaly

Real-World Use Case – GE Vernova: AWS Cost Optimization via Idle Resource Management and Rightsizing

A global energy and industrial conglomerate, **GE Vernova[1]**, realized more than **$1 million in cost savings within a year** by aggressively identifying idle or underutilized resources, shutting them down, rightsizing instances, and enforcing governance across its AWS environment.

[1] Adapted from GE *Vernova* AWS *Case Study*, in which GE used idle resource cleanup, instance scheduling, rightsizing, and modernization to save over $1 million in cloud costs. Retrieved from AWS's solutions case study on GE Vernova Amazon Web Services, Inc.

Problem: As GE prepared to become an independent entity, its cloud infrastructure costs were ballooning. The company had many **nonproduction environments, idle EC2 instances, and overprovisioned resources** that were rarely, if ever, fully utilized. GE's technology leadership needed a scalable, systematic way to trim waste while maintaining performance and future flexibility.

Approach Taken:

- **Cost Analysis and Discovery of Idle Instances:** Using AWS tools such as **Trusted Advisor**, **CloudWatch**, and internal dashboards, the cloud team identified EC2 instances and RDS databases that had very low utilization or were idle for extended periods.
- **Automated Shutdown/Scheduling for Nonproduction Resources:** GE used the **AWS Instance Scheduler** to automatically stop or start EC2 and RDS instances during non-business hours, especially in nonproduction environments. Approximately 80% of nonproduction databases were scheduled off when not in use, saving cost.
- **Decommissioning Idle Instances and Workload Rightsizing:** The team removed confirmed idle instances and right-sized others (moved them to smaller instance types or newer architectures) based on observed utilization. They also migrated some workloads to **AWS Graviton processors** for further efficiency.
- **Governance and Tagging/Reporting Enhancements:** To maintain cost control, GE improved tagging, monitoring, cost reporting, and accountability across its multiple AWS accounts. This governance framework helped prevent future drift and idle resource growth.

Impact/Benefits Achieved:

- **Over $1 million in cost savings** achieved in less than 12 months.
- **$100,000 saved** by decommissioning idle instances alone.
- **$460,000 annual savings** by scheduling down 80% of nonproduction RDS instances.
- Right-sizing and migrating to Graviton processors unlocked additional performance and savings.
- Improved infrastructure visibility, accountability, and cost governance across business units.

Lessons Learned:

- Many "hidden" costs exist in idle and underutilized resources; identifying them is the low-hanging fruit.

- Automated scheduling and shutdown policies reduce manual overhead and prevent waste.
- Rightsizing and instance modernization (for example, moving to Graviton) multiply savings beyond just resource elimination.
- Strong governance, tagging and accountability are essential to sustain cost discipline long term.

Azure Cost Management

Azure Cost Management helps organizations gain real-time visibility into their cloud spending and integrates seamlessly with Microsoft's Power BI for advanced analytics.

Key Features:

- **Budgets and Alerts:** Set spending thresholds and receive notifications when limits are exceeded. For example, you can configure an alert to notify you when your monthly spend surpasses $10,000.
- **Power BI Integration:** Build interactive visualizations to analyze trends and anomalies. Power BI allows users to create custom dashboards that combine cost data with other metrics, such as performance or security.
- **Resource Group Insights:** Break down costs by subscription, resource group, or individual service. This granularity helps identify which teams or projects are driving the most expenses.

Illustrative Use Case: Storage Tiering and Cost Optimization

Scenario: A healthcare organization reviewed its Azure storage[2] usage and found that a substantial volume of rarely accessed data was stored in high-cost **Premium** or **Hot** tiers, resulting in unnecessary expenses.

Approach:

- **Audit Storage Usage:** Identify data sets with low access frequency that were retained in performance-oriented storage tiers.

[2] Adapted from *Microsoft Azure Blog* – *"Reducing Overall Storage Costs with Azure Premium Blob Storage,"* which explores how selecting appropriate storage tiers can significantly reduce cloud expenditure based on data usage patterns. Available at: https://azure.microsoft.com/en-us/blog/reducing-overall-storage-costs-with-azure-premium-blob-storage/

- **Apply Lifecycle Policies/Tiering:** Use Azure Blob lifecycle management to migrate or schedule movement of infrequently accessed blobs to **Cool** or **Archive** tiers.
- **Monitor and Adjust:** Utilize cost analytics and alerts within Azure Cost Management to assess tiering effectiveness and fine-tune policies over time.

Hypothetical Savings: Based on average Azure tier pricing, organizations can realistically save **$10,000–$20,000 annually** by aligning storage tiers with data access frequency. Actual savings depend on total data volume, access patterns, and regional pricing models.

Lessons/Best Practices:

- Perform **regular storage audits** (monthly or quarterly) to identify cost inefficiencies.
- Implement **automated lifecycle management** to ensure consistent data tier transitions.
- Track **retrieval costs** and **access latency** to maintain a balance between cost and performance.

GCP Cost Tools

Google Cloud Platform (GCP) offers robust cost management[1] features such as Billing Reports and a Recommendations Engine.

Key Features:

- **Billing Reports:** Get detailed breakdowns of costs by project, service, or SKU. For example, you can view how much you are spending on BigQuery versus Compute Engine
- **Recommendations Engine:** Automatically identifies underutilized or idle resources. For instance, it might suggest resizing a machine type or deleting unused disks
- **Commitment Plans:** Secure discounted rates for predictable workloads through committed use contracts. Commitments can save up to 57% compared to on-demand pricing

Real-World Use Case – GCP Cost Optimization

A fast-growing startup achieved a **30% reduction in Google Cloud Platform (GCP) costs** by leveraging built-in optimization features.

Approach Taken:

- **Rightsizing Recommendations:** Adjusted over-provisioned Compute Engine instances and resized storage buckets to match actual usage patterns
- **Committed Use Discounts (CUDs):** Applied multi-year commitments for steady-state workloads, securing lower rates compared to on-demand pricing.

Benefits Achieved:

- Significant monthly cost savings without affecting application performance
- Improved resource utilization and eliminated waste
- Predictable budgeting through discounted long-term commitments

Lessons Learned:

- Continuous rightsizing ensures resources align with real demand
- Combining automated recommendations with discount programs maximizes savings potential

Real-World Use Case – ShareChat: GCP Cost Optimization via Platform Modernization and Commitment Utilization

This section explains in detail how ShareChat[3], a rapidly growing social platform, reduced cloud costs by modernizing core services and improving how committed discounts were utilized – a practical example of combining platform migration with disciplined capacity governance to get measurable savings.

Problem: ShareChat operated at a massive scale with high, variable traffic across India. As user growth surged, the engineering team needed to deliver consistent performance while keeping backend costs under control. Legacy databases and inefficient capacity planning were creating both performance and cost challenges.

Approach Taken:

1. **Platform Modernization (Cloud Spanner):** ShareChat migrated critical backend data to Cloud Spanner to gain scalable, consistent replication and reduce operational complexity. This modernization lowered the cost and

[3] Adapted from ShareChat's Google Cloud customer profile and a third-party case describing improved committed-use utilization and automated rebalancing. See: cloud.google.com customer story for ShareChat (results & Cloud Spanner migration) and a Cast.ai case write-up on how ShareChat streamlined committed-use utilization and rebalancing. https://cloud.google.com/customers/sharechat

complexity of running their global databases while improving availability and performance.

2. **Improve Committed-Spend Utilization and Rightsizing**: To make commitment discounts work for them, ShareChat focused on improving utilization of committed spend and on automated rebalancing of node types and pools (so commitments covered actual usage more effectively). They used automation/rebalancing to reduce wasted capacity and ensure commitments mapped to real consumption patterns.

3. **Continuous Monitoring and Governance**: ShareChat implemented monitoring and cost-governance practices that tracked request volumes, storage/compute utilization, and commitment coverage – enabling the team to adjust capacity and commitments as demand shifted.

Benefits/Impact:

- ~30% reduction in costs attributed to the move to Cloud Spanner and the efficiencies it unlocked (better replication model and lower operational overhead).
- Significantly improved scalability (ShareChat handles billions of requests per day) with lower cost-per-user at scale.
- Further downstream savings and operational efficiency gains by improving utilization of committed spend and automating cluster/node rebalancing (reportedly driving material additional savings and reducing manual effort).

Lessons/Best Practices:

- Modernizing stateful systems (for example, to Cloud Spanner) can both raise reliability and reduce total cost of ownership for large, distributed workloads.
- Buying committed discounts is only half the story – you must actively maximize utilization (by rightsizing, rebalancing, and matching commitments to real usage) to realize the full benefit.
- Automation (node rebalancing, autoscaling, and commit-analysis dashboards) converts commitment discounts into predictable, repeatable savings with less operational toil.

Cost Management Setup: AWS Cost Explorer vs. GCP Billing vs. FinOps Best Practices

A strategic cloud cost management setup requires evaluating the native tooling of major providers, such as AWS Cost Explorer and the Google Cloud Billing console, against the cross-functional principles of the FinOps framework.

Aspect	AWS Cost Explorer	GCP Billing	FinOps Best Practices
Purpose	Visualize, analyze, and forecast AWS spending	Track, analyze, and optimize GCP usage and costs	Establish visibility, accountability, and continuous optimization across clouds
Access	`AWS Management Console → Billing & Cost Management → Cost Explorer`	`Google Cloud Console → Billing → Reports`	Centralized dashboard (for example, CloudHealth, Apptio, Stacklet) for multi-cloud visibility
Key Features	• Cost and usage reports • Forecasting • Rightsizing recommendations • Savings Plans/RI tracking	• Custom billing reports • Budget alerts • Committed Use Discounts (CUDs) • Export to BigQuery for analysis	• Tagging enforcement • Policy-as-Code (PaC) • Chargeback/ showback models • Automation via FinOps as Code (FaC)
Setup Steps	1. Enable Cost and Usage Reports (CUR) in the Billing console 2. Define cost allocation tags (example Project, Team, Env) 3. Use Cost Explorer to create reports by service, region, or tag 4. Set up budgets and alerts via AWS Budgets	1. Link billing account to projects 2. Enable billing export to BigQuery 3. Create custom reports using Project, Label, SKU 4. Set budgets and alerts in Cloud Billing	1. Implement mandatory tagging policy. 2. Integrate with IaC tools (Terraform, CloudFormation) 3. Deploy Policy-as-Code (OPA, Cloud Custodian) 4. Automate cost reviews and reporting
Cost Allocation	Tags + Resource Groups for team/project spend tracking	Labels + Billing Accounts for department/product tracking	Enforce tagging/ labeling via automation to block untagged deployments

Forecasting	12-month forecast from historical trends	Predictive forecasting in Cloud Billing	Combine forecasting with Savings Plans/ CUDs for long-term optimization
Budget Alerts	AWS Budgets: Threshold alerts (example 80%) via SNS	Cloud Billing Budgets: Alerts when spend exceeds limits	Automated Slack/ Teams alerts + CI/CD integration
Rightsizing & Optimization	Built-in instance rightsizing recommendations	VM optimization suggestions from usage metrics	Automated tools (Stacklet, CloudHealth) for underutilized resource detection
Automation & Governance	Limited native automation; use AWS Config + Lambda or SCPs	Use Organization Policies + Terraform for enforcement	FinOps as Code: Automated cost governance with tools like Stacklet (Cloud Custodian) to **`inform`** → **`warn`** → **`block`**
Real-World Example	Retailer saved 6% by shutting down idle non-prod resources	SaaS provider optimized CUDs after BigQuery analysis	Avalara achieved **500% ROI**, 30–60% lower run rates, and 80% less manual work with automated policy enforcement[4]
Integration with IaC	Works with Terraform, CloudFormation via tagging policies	Works with Terraform, Deployment Manager	Embed cost checks in PRs via OPA/Stacklet before deployment
Self-Service Visibility	AWS console; export to CSV/Quicksight	Export to BigQuery for SQL-based analytics	Stacklet AssetDB: Engineers query cloud assets in real-time
Multi-Cloud Support	AWS-only	GCP-only	Third-party tools (CloudHealth, Apptio, Stacklet) for unified multi-cloud management

Table 6.1: *Cloud Cost Management Tool Comparison*

[4] Adapted from Stacklet – *Avalara Unlocks Cloud Savings and Improves Engineer Experience with Automated Cost Governance*. Retrieved from https://stacklet.io/case-study/avalara-unlocks-cloud-savings-and-improves-engineer-experience-with-automated-cost-governance

This table provides a detailed comparison between native cloud provider tools (AWS Cost Explorer, GCP Billing) and FinOps best practices for comprehensive cloud financial management.

Third-Party FinOps Platforms

Native tools give you visibility, while **third-party platforms give you strategy**. By unifying data across AWS, Azure, and GCP, these solutions deliver **multi-cloud insights, advanced automation, and consistent governance** that native tools alone cannot provide. The result is a smarter strategy for cost control, which leads to stronger compliance with rules and faster decision-making.

Apptio Cloudability

Beyond the capabilities of native tools, many organizations turn to advanced platforms like Cloudability to **gain deeper visibility, streamline governance, and drive continuous optimization**. Apptio Cloudability stands out for its multi-cloud visibility and automation capabilities. It provides a unified view of spending across AWS, Azure, GCP, and other providers, enabling organizations to manage costs holistically.

Key Features:

- **Multi-Cloud Support:** Gain a unified view of spending across multiple cloud providers. This is particularly valuable for organizations operating in multi-cloud environments.
- **Automation:** Automate tasks like shutting down idle instances or resizing resources. For example, you can schedule scripts to terminate unused instances during off-hours.
- **Advanced Analytics:** Leverage machine learning to uncover hidden savings opportunities. The platform analyzes usage patterns and recommends optimizations tailored to your workload.

Real-World Use Case - Multi-Cloud Cost Optimization with Automated Governance

Avalara[1] reduced its cloud spend by **25%** by implementing automated resource lifecycle management and enforcing strict tagging policies across all environments.

Approach Taken:

- **Automated Decommissioning:** Created workflows to detect and retire unused resources in near real time, minimizing idle infrastructure costs

- **Tagging Policy Enforcement:** Applied mandatory tags to all new deployments, enabling precise cost allocation to projects and departments
- **Cross-Cloud Governance:** Integrated policies across AWS, Azure, and GCP to maintain consistent cost management practices

Benefits Achieved:

- Substantial cost savings without sacrificing service quality
- Greater visibility and accountability for cloud usage
- Streamlined governance processes that reduced manual oversight

Lessons Learned:

- Automation eliminates delays and human error in cost-control measures
- Consistent tagging is essential for accurate budgeting and chargebacks

CloudHealth by VMware

CloudHealth focuses on governance and policy enforcement to help organizations optimize cloud costs.

Key Features:

- **Policy Enforcement:** Prevent costly behaviors by setting rules around resource provisioning. For example, you can restrict the creation of oversized instances unless explicitly approved.
- **Governance:** Ensure compliance with best practices and internal cost allocation strategies. The platform provides templates and guidelines for implementing governance frameworks.
- **Security Monitoring:** Identify vulnerabilities that could impact both security and cost efficiency. For instance, unencrypted storage or public-facing databases might incur additional risks and costs.

Real-World Use Case: A global retail chain streamlined its multi-cloud strategy by standardizing tagging practices and enforcing cost governance policies. They reduced costs by 18% and improved visibility into cloud spending across departments.

Spot.io

Spot.io specializes in maximizing cost efficiency through the use of spot instances and reserved capacity.

Key Features:

- **Spot Instances:** Reduce compute costs by up to 90% by leveraging temporary, discounted resources. Spot instances are ideal for batch processing, CI/CD pipelines, and other non-critical workloads.

- **Reserved Capacity:** Optimize predictable workloads with committed use discounts. For example, you can reserve capacity for steady-state applications like databases or web servers.
- **Automation:** Dynamically adjust resource allocation based on workload demands. The platform dynamically analyzes real-time usage and proactively optimizes configurations to minimize waste.

Real-World Use Case – Epic Games: Cloud Cost Optimization with Spot and Reserved Instances

Epic Games[5], the developer behind *Fortnite* and the Unreal Engine, optimized its cloud compute costs by employing a hybrid cost strategy on AWS. The company combined **Spot Instances** for non-critical tasks with **Reserved Instances** for essential services, thereby lowering expenses while preserving performance for its global user base.

Approach Taken:

- **Spot Instance Adoption:** Epic deployed **EC2 Spot Instances** for workloads that could tolerate interruptions–such as automated testing, analytics jobs, content pipelines, and build environments. This allowed them to take advantage of significantly discounted rates compared to On-Demand instances.
- **Reserved Capacity Planning:** For always-on services (game servers, matchmaking, back-end infrastructure), Epic committed to **Reserved Instances** (with multi-year terms). This ensured reliable availability and predictable billing for critical systems.
- **Workload Segmentation:** The team categorized workloads by criticality and required uptime. Mission-critical services ran on reserved capacity, while batch, experimental, or auxiliary tasks ran on Spot capacity–optimizing cost vs. reliability tradeoffs.
- **Monitoring and Governance:** Through AWS Cost Explorer, utilization metrics, and internal dashboards, Epic continually evaluated instance performance, interruption risk, and cost benefit. This feedback loop enabled adjustments to the balance between Spot and Reserved allocations over time.

---

[5] Epic Games has built *Fortnite*'s backend infrastructure on AWS, relying heavily on **Amazon EC2** for its global, scalable compute needs. As part of its cloud governance strategy, Epic reported that it reduced cloud spend by about **20 percent** through improved resource visibility, governance, and optimization across its EC2 usage. Amazon Web Services, Inc.

Benefits Achieved:

- Up to **20 % reduction in overall cloud spend** (as publicly reported by Epic's governance team)
- Enhanced ability to **scale elastically** during peak demand (for example, new content drops or in-game events)
- Maintained **consistent player experience** by preserving mission-critical infrastructure on reserved capacity
- Better **cost visibility and governance**, leading to smarter decision-making about resource allocation

Lessons Learned:

- Spot Instances are powerful cost savers when used for workloads that can tolerate occasional termination.
- A hybrid strategy – combining Spot and Reserved capacity – strikes a balanced compromise between cost and reliability.
- Continuous monitoring and cost governance are essential to prevent overspending or misallocation.
- Proper tagging, workload classification, and feedback loops help maintain an evolving optimal allocation strategy.

Comparison Table – Native Tools vs. Third-Party Tools

Selecting the right tooling is critical for cloud financial management, requiring a clear understanding of the trade-offs between the native solutions offered by cloud providers and the advanced, cross-platform capabilities of dedicated third-party FinOps platforms.

Feature / Capability	**Native Cloud Cost Tools (AWS Cost Explorer, Azure Cost Management, GCP Billing)**	**Third-Party FinOps Platforms (Cloudability, Apptio, Spot.io)**
Cloud Provider Scope	Single-cloud (provider-specific)	Multi-cloud visibility across AWS, Azure, GCP, and so on
Automation	Limited to provider features	Advanced automation (shutdowns, rightsizing, policy enforcement)
Analytics Depth	Standard dashboards and usage reports	Predictive analytics, AI-based optimization

Integration	Tight integration with provider ecosystem	Broad integrations (ITSM, DevOps, CI/CD pipelines)
Customization	Limited to native configurations	Highly customizable dashboards, alerts, and reports
Cost	Often free or bundled with cloud services	Separate licensing costs but may yield higher ROI

***Table 6.2**: FinOps Tool Selection Matrix*

This matrix compares the primary categories of FinOps tools to help organizations select the right solutions based on their specific requirements and constraints.

Rightsizing Decision Flowchart

Flow:

1. **Identify underutilized resources** → Check CPU, memory, network usage
2. **Classify workload type** → Steady-state or variable usage
3. **Decision:**
    - If **steady-state**, consider Reserved Instances or Committed Use Discounts
    - If **variable**, apply Auto-Scaling or Spot Instances
4. **Test in staging** before implementing in production
5. **Monitor post-change** to validate cost and performance improvements

Tagging Strategy Matrix

A well-defined tagging strategy is fundamental to cloud cost allocation and accountability, serving as the critical link between raw resource data and meaningful business insights.

Tag Key	**Example Value**	**Purpose**	**Owner/Enforced By**
Environment	Dev, Test, Prod	Enables environment-based cost tracking	DevOps / Cloud Governance
Project	Carbon Calculator	Maps spend to specific initiatives	Project Managers
CostCenter	Finance, R&D	Aligns costs to budget owners	Finance Team

Region	eu-west-1, us-east-1	Supports compliance and latency management	Cloud Architects
Owner	j.smith@example.com	Accountability for resource lifecycle	Resource Creator / Manager

***Table 6.3**: Essential Tagging Strategy Matrix*

This matrix outlines the core tags required for effective cloud cost management, accountability, and governance.

Advanced Strategies for Cloud Cost Optimization

You have mastered the basics and now, it is time to unlock the next level.

In this section, we will focus on automation, predictive analytics, and following FinOps best practices to keep costs low **while** scaling rapidly. The goal: make every cloud dollar deliver maximum business value.

Rightsizing Resources

Rightsizing involves adjusting cloud resources to match actual workload requirements. Overprovisioned resources can lead to significant waste, while under provisioned resources may cause performance bottlenecks. Tools like GCP Recommendations Engine and AWS Trusted Advisor help identify opportunities for rightsizing.

Steps to Implement Rightsizing

1. Analyze usage patterns using native or third-party tools. Look for instances that are consistently underutilized or overutilized.
2. Adjust instance sizes or storage capacities to match workload demands. For example, you might downgrade a large instance to a medium instance if CPU utilization is consistently low.
3. Monitor performance post-adjustment to ensure no degradation occurs. Use monitoring tools to verify that the changes haven't negatively impacted application performance.

Example: A media streaming service reduced its monthly AWS bill by 15% by downsizing oversized RDS instances.

Reserved Instances and Savings Plans

Reserved Instances (RIs) and Savings Plans allow organizations to commit to specific usage levels in exchange for significant discounts. These options are ideal for predictable workloads.

Key Considerations:

- Evaluate workload stability before committing to RIs or Savings Plans. For example, if your workload fluctuates frequently, you might prefer on-demand pricing instead
- Regularly review utilization to ensure commitments align with actual usage. Tools like AWS Cost Explorer and Azure Cost Management can help track RI utilization

Real-World Use Case – SmugMug: Storage Cost Optimization via Amazon S3 (Contextual)

SmugMug[6], the parent of Flickr and a prominent SaaS image-hosting platform, used AWS technologies (including Amazon S3 and later EC2) to optimize its infrastructure costs and scale its operations cost-effectively. While this example centers more on storage than compute, it demonstrates how commitment to cloud services enabled significant cost savings and operational agility. The following narrative integrates the SmugMug example to illustrate how cloud-based adoption yields savings when compared to traditional infrastructure.

Approach/Transition Undertaken

- **Migration to Amazon S3 storage:** SmugMug moved a large portion of its image storage from on-premises hardware (disk arrays and servers) to Amazon S3. This allowed them to offload hardware, maintenance, and scaling costs.
- **Cost Avoidance and Growth Planning:** Prior to S3, SmugMug was investing ~$40,000 per month in hardware and storage infrastructure and expected that to grow to ~$80,000/month as usage expanded. SmugMug's Don MacAskill

  By using S3, they avoided incremental capital and operational costs, including power, cooling, hardware replacement, and administrative overhead. Over seven months, they reported cumulative cost avoidance of ~$423,686.75 vs. ~$84,255.25 spent on S3, leading to net savings. SmugMug's Don MacAskill

[6] Don MacAskill, "Amazon S3: Show me the money," SmugMug blog, November 10, 2006. Retrieved from https://don.blogs.smugmug.com/2006/11/10/amazon-s3-show-me-the-money/

They projected further annual savings of over $500,000 if growth continued. SmugMug's Don MacAskill

- **Integrating EC2 and Cloud Services:** Although the blog post focuses on storage, SmugMug also mentions that EC2 usage is in their roadmap and that parts of their architecture depend on Amazon's compute services. SmugMug's Don MacAskill

Impact/Benefits Observed

- **Substantial cost avoidance** when compared to the costs of scaling internal storage systems
- Ability to **scale storage transparently** without tying capital to hardware
- Reduced operational burden (hardware maintenance, lifecycle management)
- Freed up resources to focus on core product development and customer experience

Limitations/Lessons Learned

- The SmugMug example is from **2006** to **2007**, so the cost models, AWS pricing, and cloud maturity have evolved since then.
- As a blog post, the data is self-reported and not audited.
- The focus is primarily on storage, not compute or cross-service cost optimization.

Tagging Best Practices

While implementing a tagging strategy is the first step, its long-term effectiveness and accuracy depend entirely on adhering to a consistent set of governance rules.

Tagging is a foundational practice for effective cloud cost management. Tags help categorize resources, enabling granular tracking and allocation of costs.

Best Practices for Tagging:

1. Define a consistent tagging schema across all cloud environments. For example, use tags like "`Environment=Production`" or "`Department=Marketing`."
2. Enforce mandatory tagging policies for new resources. Many cloud providers allow you to block deployments that lack required tags.
3. Use automated tools to retroactively tag untagged resources. For instance, you can run scripts to apply default tags to existing resources.

Real-World Use Case – Siemens: Automating Cloud Cost Allocation through Tagging

Siemens AG [71], a global industrial and technology powerhouse operating in more than 200 countries, faced increasing challenges in tracking and allocating cloud costs across its diverse business units. With thousands of AWS accounts supporting various digital products and IoT solutions, manual cost allocation became inefficient and error-prone.

In 2022, Siemens' Cloud Center of Excellence (CCoE) launched an initiative to **standardize cost tagging and automate allocation reporting** across all AWS environments.

Approach Taken:

- **Tagging Framework Implementation:** Siemens introduced a unified tagging taxonomy—covering project ID, cost center, owner, and environment—that applied across EC2, S3, RDS, and Lambda resources. AWS Config and Service Control Policies (SCPs) enforced compliance with the tagging standards.
- **Automation and Governance:** Using **AWS Organizations, Cost Explorer, and AWS Budgets**, Siemens automated the roll-up of cost data per business unit, allowing finance teams to see near real-time spend distribution without manual reconciliation.
- **Change Management and Training:** The CCoE trained over 300 engineers across multiple departments to ensure consistent tag application and reporting accuracy.

Impact/Benefits Achieved:

- **50% reduction in manual effort** for cost allocation and financial reporting
- Improved visibility into **cost drivers across 20+ global business units**
- Streamlined budgeting and accountability between technical and finance teams
- Established a reusable governance model for new AWS workloads

Lessons Learned:

- A **centralized tagging policy** dramatically simplifies financial transparency in multi-account environments.
- **Automation and compliance enforcement** prevent drift and missing tags over time.

[7] Adapted from AWS *Customer Success Stories – Siemens builds governance and cost transparency with* AWS *Organizations and tagging best practices*. Retrieved from https://aws.amazon.com/solutions/case-studies/innovators/siemens/

- Collaboration between technical and finance teams is critical to ensure the tagging framework aligns with real business structures.

Building Dashboards for Enhanced Visibility

Effective cloud cost management starts with visibility. Native cloud tools and third-party platforms enable organizations to build dashboards that provide clear insights into spending patterns.

Key Features

- **Real-Time Monitoring:** Track live cost metrics to stay ahead of budget overruns
- **Custom Reports:** Tailor reports to focus on specific services, teams, or projects
- **Automated Alerts:** Receive instant notifications when spending exceeds predefined thresholds

Best Practices for Dashboard Configuration:

1. **Define Key Metrics:** Focus on spend trends, usage efficiency, and cost allocation
2. **Enable Tagging:** Use tags to categorize resources and track costs accurately
3. **Automate Reporting:** Schedule weekly or monthly reports to keep stakeholders

Cultural Shift Towards FinOps

Implementing FinOps successfully requires moving beyond a technical or financial initiative to become a true organizational mindset. The core cultural shift involves transitioning from a model of isolated accountability to one of shared ownership, where cloud cost efficiency becomes a collective KPI across the business.

This means embedding cost consciousness into the daily workflow of every team that influences cloud consumption:

- Product Managers now weigh feature benefits against their infrastructure run-rate, making trade-offs between innovation velocity and unit economics.
- Security and Compliance Teams collaborate on governance policies that are both secure and cost-aware, ensuring that compliance does not lead to over-provisioned resources by default.

- Leadership sets the tone by incentivizing efficiency and celebrating cost-saving innovations with the same enthusiasm as feature launches.

Ultimately, this cultural evolution positions the cloud not as an opaque utility bill, but as a dynamic, manageable resource that everyone is empowered to optimize.

Steps to Foster a FinOps Culture

Establishing a sustainable FinOps practice requires a systematic approach that transforms cloud financial management from a periodic audit into an integrated business discipline. Organizations can accelerate this cultural shift through several key initiatives:

1. Educate teams about the importance of cost optimization
2. Establish clear roles and responsibilities for managing cloud costs
3. Celebrate successes and share lessons learned to encourage continuous improvement

Measuring Success in FinOps

To measure the success of FinOps initiatives, organizations should track key performance indicators (KPIs). Some examples include:

- Percentage reduction in cloud costs year-over-year
- Number of idle resources identified and eliminated
- Time taken to resolve cost anomalies

By regularly reviewing these KPIs, organizations can assess the effectiveness of their FinOps efforts to make data-driven decisions.

Conclusion

Mastering cloud cost management is a journey that requires ongoing effort and collaboration. By leveraging native cloud tools, third-party platforms, and advanced strategies like rightsizing and tagging, organizations can achieve significant cost savings while maintaining operational excellence. The next chapter explains how automation revolutionizes FinOps.

Key Terms

- **FinOps:** Financial operations for cloud cost management
- **Cloud Cost Allocation:** Assigning cloud costs to different teams or projects
- Rightsizing: Adjusting cloud resources to match workload requirements

- Spot Instances: Temporary, discounted cloud compute resources
- Tagging: Labeling cloud resources for better tracking

Points to Remember

- Use native cost management tools for real-time insights.
- Third-party FinOps tools provide multi-cloud support and automation.
- Dashboards are essential for visibility and proactive cost control.
- Automation helps prevent waste and optimize resource usage.

Questions

1. What are the key features of AWS Cost Explorer?
2. How does Azure Cost Management integrate with Power BI?
3. What is the main advantage of using Spot Instances?
4. How does CloudHealth help enforce cost governance?
5. Why is tagging important in cloud cost management?

Multiple Choice Questions

1. Which of the following tools provides multi-cloud cost visibility?
   a. AWS Cost Explorer
   b. Azure Cost Management
   c. Apptio Cloudability
   d. GCP Billing Reports
2. What is a primary feature of Spot.io?
   a. Cost forecasting
   b. Automated use of spot instances
   c. Security compliance monitoring
   d. Power BI integration

3. Which of the following is NOT a benefit of tagging?
    a. Improved cost allocation
    b. Enhanced security monitoring
    c. Increased resource utilization
    d. Simplified reporting
4. What is the main purpose of Reserved Instances?
    a. Real-time cost monitoring
    b. Discounted rates for predictable workloads
    c. Automated resource scaling
    d. Multi-cloud visibility
5. Which platform specializes in governance and policy enforcement?
    a. AWS Cost Explorer
    b. CloudHealth by VMware
    c. Spot.io
    d. Azure Cost Management

Answers

1. c
2. b
3. c
4. b
5. b

Scenario-Based Questions

1. Your organization operates workloads across **AWS**, **Azure**, and **GCP**, and needs a single platform to track spending, enforce tagging policies, and recommend cost optimizations.
2. Your finance team notices that several virtual machines in non-production environments have been running overnight and during weekends across

multiple clouds. They want an **automated solution** that can shut them down based on schedule and generate monthly cost reports.

3. You have a workload on AWS that experiences **predictable, steady usage** throughout the year. Which cost optimization strategy is most suitable to reduce compute costs without changing the architecture of the workload?
4. A startup wants to begin cost governance without investing in additional tools. They want to track usage, set budgets, and generate forecasts **within their cloud provider's ecosystem**. Which approach should they take first?
5. Your company stores a large amount of data in **premium storage tiers** on Azure, but most of it is rarely accessed. What is the most effective way to reduce costs while maintaining data availability?

Answers

1. **Third-party FinOps Platform** (for example, Apptio Cloudability, Flexera, Spot.io): Native tools are siloed; third-party platforms give unified multi-cloud visibility and governance
2. **Automated Resource Lifecycle Management:** Schedules idle resource shutdowns and generates cost reports automatically
3. **Committed Use Discounts (CUDs) or AWS Savings Plans:** Locks in lower rates for steady workloads without changing architecture
4. **Use Native Cost Management Tools** (AWS Cost Explorer, Azure Cost Management + Billing, GCP Billing Reports): Free, built-in tools for tracking usage, budgets, and forecasts
5. **Migrate Data to Cold or Archive Storage Tiers:** Reduces costs for infrequently accessed data without deleting it

CHAPTER 7
Introduction to Automation in FinOps

Introduction

Imagine managing the finances of a bustling city where every streetlight, public transport route, and park requires funding. Without proper oversight, costs can spiral out of control, leading to inefficiencies and wasted resources. Similarly, cloud environments face a comparable challenge: thousands of resources spin up, scale, and shut down dynamically every day. Without proper governance, these resources can lead to spiraling costs, inefficiencies, and budget overruns.

The complexity of modern cloud environments demands a new approach to financial management that blends technology, data, and collaboration to optimize spending while driving innovation. This is where FinOps (Financial Operations) comes into play. FinOps bridges the gap between finance, engineering, and leadership to ensure that cloud investments align with business priorities.

This chapter will explore how automation revolutionizes FinOps by blending technical solutions with cultural shifts. We will delve into practical examples, tools, and strategies that turn cost management from a reactive chore into a proactive superpower. Whether you are a developer tasked with optimizing cloud spending or a finance professional looking to bridge the gap with engineering teams, this chapter will equip you with the knowledge and tools to thrive in the evolving world of cloud financial management.

Structure

By the end of this chapter, you will understand:

- How automation transforms key aspects of FinOps, such as tagging, forecasting, and lifecycle management
- The tools and techniques used to implement automation effectively
- Real-world use cases demonstrating the impact of automation in FinOps

- Strategies to overcome common challenges and drive cultural change within your organization

Understanding Automation in FinOps

Automation in FinOps transforms chaotic cloud spending into clarity by streamlining repetitive tasks, enforcing governance policies, and providing actionable insights. It empowers teams to innovate responsibly while maintaining financial discipline. Think of automation as giving your engineers a GPS for cloud spending to provide real-time guidance, enforce smarter decisions, and encounter fewer budgeting headaches.

By automating processes such as tagging, forecasting, and lifecycle management, FinOps ensures that every dollar spent aligns with organizational goals such as growth, innovation, or sustainability via the following processes:

- **Tagging:** Automating metadata assignment to track resource ownership and usage
- **Forecasting:** Predicting future costs based on historical trends to avoid surprises
- **Lifecycle Management:** Automating the creation, scaling, and termination of resources to prevent waste

Why Automation Matters in FinOps

In today's fast-paced digital landscape, manual processes are no longer sufficient. Human error, inconsistent practices, and lack of visibility can lead to significant financial losses. Automation addresses these challenges by:

- **Reducing Manual Effort:** Freeing teams from repetitive tasks so they can focus on high-impact work
- **Improving Accuracy:** Ensuring consistent application of policies and reducing errors
- **Enhancing Visibility:** Providing real-time insights into resource usage and spending patterns
- **Driving Accountability:** Enforcing governance policies programmatically to ensure compliance

Amazon leveraged automation to optimize its cloud infrastructure during peak demand periods. By implementing robotic systems in its fulfillment centers, Amazon achieved a 25% reduction in operational costs at its Shreveport, Louisiana facility. This automation allowed the company to dynamically adjust resources based on real-time demand, ensuring efficient scaling and significant cost savings. Financial Tim

Automating Tagging and Resource Management

Effective tagging is the cornerstone of any successful FinOps practice. Metadata labels applied to cloud resources called tags enable organizations to track ownership, purpose, environment, and cost allocation across teams and projects. Without consistent tagging, cloud spend becomes opaque, making it nearly impossible to assign accountability or optimize usage.

FinOps Tip: Use Policy-as-Code to enforce tagging consistency at scale and reduce compliance risks. Automated guardrails such as AWS Config rules, Azure Policy, or GCP Organization Policies, can prevent untagged resources from being deployed. This proactive enforcement ensures that every new resource inherits required tags (for example, **`cost-center`**, **`project`**, **`owner`**), while maintaining data integrity from day one.

Common Pitfall: Relying on manual tagging audits leads to inconsistent metadata and hidden costs. "Untagged resources are like mystery charges on a credit card statement–they create distrust," says **Sasi Kanumuri**, a FinOps practitioner and author of the blog post *FinOps- Cloud Tagging- Tagging* 101. AWS in Plain English, In his experience, untagged resources lead to hours of manual investigation, finger-pointing between teams, and lost visibility into which projects drive value. For example, an untagged EC2 instance running unnecessarily could cost thousands of dollars monthly without anyone knowing its purpose. Manual tagging is not only labor-intensive but also prone to errors, leading to incomplete or inconsistent metadata.

The human cost of manual tagging extends far beyond wasted time. It creates friction between teams, erodes trust, and hinders decision-making. Without clear attribution, stakeholders struggle to understand resource usage patterns, making it difficult to allocate budgets effectively. This lack of visibility can also impact compliance efforts, especially in industries with strict regulatory requirements like healthcare or finance.

Consider the following scenarios:

- **Finance Teams:** Unable to attribute costs to specific departments or projects, finance teams struggle to generate accurate budget reports.
- **Engineering Teams:** Engineers waste valuable time investigating unattributed costs instead of focusing on innovation.
- **Leadership:** Executives lack the insights needed to make informed decisions about resource allocation and strategic investments.

For example, imagine a marketing team running a campaign on AWS. If the associated EC2 instances and S3 buckets are not tagged properly, the costs of the campaign might be lumped with general IT expenses. This makes it impossible to measure the

ROI of the campaign, leading to poor decision-making and potential budget cuts for future initiatives.

Manual tagging also introduces risks during audits. In regulated industries like healthcare or finance, failing to tag resources properly can result in non-compliance penalties. For instance, a healthcare provider might fail HIPAA audits if patient data is not clearly attributed to compliant resources.

Lifecycle Management: Right-Sizing Resources Across Their Journey

Cloud resources have a lifecycle–from provisioning and active use to underutilization and eventual decommissioning. Effective lifecycle management ensures that resources are appropriately sized, utilized, and retired in a timely manner, avoiding unnecessary spend on idle or over-provisioned infrastructure.

FinOps Tip: Implement automated right-sizing and shutdown policies based on utilization metrics to reduce waste. Tools such as AWS Compute Optimizer, Azure Advisor, or GCP Recommender analyze historical usage patterns (for example, CPU, memory, network) to recommend optimal instance types or identify candidates for shutdown. Automating these recommendations through scheduled actions or orchestration workflows ensures continuous optimization with minimal manual intervention.

Common Pitfall: Treating cloud resources as "set-and-forget" leads to zombie assets and cost bloat. Many organizations provision resources for short-term projects but fail to decommission them afterward. A development environment spun up for a sprint may remain active for months, incurring costs with zero business value. These "zombie" resources, such as idle VMs, orphaned disks, or unused load balancers are a major source of waste. One enterprise found that 30% of its cloud expenditure was spent on underutilized or abandoned resources.

Moreover, over-provisioning remains a common issue. Teams often choose larger instance types "just to be safe," leading to significant underutilization. For example, an **`m5.xlarge`** instance running at 10% average CPU utilization for six months could have been replaced with a smaller instance, saving over $1,000 annually.

As discussed earlier, automated tagging plays a crucial role since without accurate **`environment`**, **`project`**, and **`owner`** tags, identifying and notifying the right stakeholders for cleanup becomes nearly impossible.

Proactive lifecycle management is not just about cost savings, but about agility. Regular cleanup cycles free up capacity, reduce security risks, and improve operational clarity. FinOps teams should establish clear policies for resource expiration (for example, auto-delete after 90 days unless renewed) and integrate lifecycle reviews into sprint retrospectives or quarterly planning.

Forecasting: Predicting Spend to Drive Business Outcomes

Accurate forecasting enables organizations to anticipate cloud costs, align budgets with business goals, and avoid billing surprises. Unlike traditional IT, where capital expenditures are predictable, cloud's variable consumption model demands dynamic forecasting models that reflect actual usage trends.

FinOps Tip: Combine historical spend data with business drivers (for example, user growth, feature launches) to build scenario-based forecasts. Use tools like AWS Cost Explorer, Azure Cost Management, or third-party platforms to analyze past trends and project future spend. Then layer in business context–such as upcoming product releases or marketing campaigns–to create realistic high/low/mid-range forecasts. This approach bridges finance and engineering, enabling data-driven conversations about trade-offs and priorities.

Common Pitfall: Relying solely on historical trends ignores business velocity and leads to inaccurate forecasts. A common mistake is extrapolating last month's expenditure into the future without considering upcoming changes. For example, a company planning a major app release that will double traffic should expect infrastructure costs to rise, but basing it on a purely historical model might miss this nuance entirely. Conversely, teams may overestimate growth and over-provision, leading to wasted capacity.

A SaaS company learned this the hard way when their CFO approved a $500,000 budget based on flat historical growth. Two weeks after launch, their user base tripled and so did their cloud bill. Without a scenario-based forecast, they faced a $200K overspend and had to scramble for emergency funding.

Forecasting should be a collaborative and iterative process involving engineering, product, and finance teams. Regular forecast reviews (for example, monthly or quarterly) can refine assumptions and improve accuracy over time. Additionally, setting up anomaly detection alerts can flag unexpected spikes early, allowing for rapid investigation and adjustment.

Note: *Forecasting is not about predicting the future perfectly–it is about reducing uncertainty and empowering better decisions.*

How Automation Builds Accountability

Automation makes cost, usage, and compliance data transparent to all stakeholders.

This shared visibility ensures teams take ownership of their actions and align decisions with organizational goals.

Automation: Eliminating Manual Chaos with Policy as Code

```
policies:
- name: tag-untagged-resources
  resource: aws.*
  filters:
    - "tag:Owner": absent
  actions:
    - type: tag
      key: Owner
      value: "cloud-admin@company.com"
    - type: notify
      to: #slack-finops-alerts
      template: |
        {account_id}: {resource_type} {resource_id} missing Owner tag.
        Default tag applied. Review: {link_to_console}
```

Figure 7.1: *Policy as Code*

The policy will:

- Apply to all AWS resources (**`aws.*`**)
- Filter for resources missing the "**`Owner`**" tag
- Tag those resources with "**`Owner: cloud-admin@company.com`**"
- Send a notification to the Slack channel with details about the resource

Manual tagging is error-prone, inconsistent, and unsustainable at scale. Automation eliminates this chaos by enforcing tagging policies programmatically. Tools such as Terraform, Azure Policy, and AWS Config enable organizations to define governance rules as code, ensuring that every resource is properly tagged before it is even deployed.

This approach, known as Policy as Code, transforms cloud governance from a reactive, compliance-driven effort into a proactive, integrated part of the development lifecycle. By codifying tagging requirements, teams ensure consistency, reduce risk, and build accountability directly into infrastructure provisioning.

FinOps Tip: Embed tagging policies into Infrastructure as Code (IaC) templates to enforce compliance at deployment time. Preventing any misconfiguration before it happens is far more effective than trying to fix it later. When tagging rules are baked into Terraform modules or CloudFormation templates, every new resource automatically inherits required tags where no human intervention is needed. This shift-left approach ensures that cost visibility is built into the foundation of your cloud environment.

Common Pitfall: Applying tagging policies only *after* resources are deployed leads to coverage gaps and technical debt. Many organizations attempt to "clean up" tagging after the fact using scripts or manual audits. But this is like mopping the floor while the tap is still running. Without automated enforcement at the source, new untagged resources will continue to appear faster than they can be corrected. Teams end up in a constant cycle of catch-up, especially in dynamic environments with high deployment velocity.

For example, a fintech startup tried to retroactively tag all AWS resources monthly. But with hundreds of new instances launched weekly through CI/CD pipelines, their tagging coverage never exceeded the 60% threshold. It was not until they enforced tagging in Terraform that compliance became sustainable.

Policy as Code Example: Healthcare Compliance Made Automated

A healthcare company uses Terraform to mandate tags for HIPAA compliance, ensuring all resources handling patient data are fully auditable. Here is how it works:

```
# Enforce mandatory tags in Terraform
resource "azurerm_resource_group" "example" {
  name     = "medical-data-rg"
  location = "East US"

  tags = {
    project     = var.project_name
    owner       = var.owner_email
    compliance  = "HIPAA"
    environment = var.environment
    cost-center = var.cost_center
  }
}
```

***Figure* 7.2**: *Enforcing Mandatory Tags in Terraform*

This configuration creates an Azure Resource Group with mandatory tags for:

- Project identification
- Owner contact
- HIPAA compliance marking
- Environment classification
- Cost center tracking

The use of variables (`var.*`) makes this template reusable across different deployments while enforcing consistent tagging practices.

A validation rule in the CI/CD pipeline checks that all Terraform plans include these tags. If a developer omits a required field (for example, **`compliance`**), the deployment fails automatically.

FinOps Tip: Use pre-deployment validation in CI/CD to stop non-compliant infrastructure before it reaches production. Integrating policy checks into pipelines (via tools like Open Policy Agent (OPA), Checkov, or HashiCorp Sentinel) ensures that governance scales with development speed. These tools can evaluate IaC against organizational standards and block deployments that violate tagging, security, or cost policies.

Common Pitfall: Assuming tagging enforcement ends at deployment–ignoring configuration drift over time. Even if resources start to be compliant, they can become non-compliant later. For example, an engineer might manually add a resource via the AWS Console that bypasses Terraform, creating a gap in tagging and compliance. This is known as configuration drift.

To combat this, combine *preventive* controls (such as IaC enforcement) with *detective* and *corrective* controls (such as AWS Config rules or Azure Policy in **`"audit"`** or **`"deny"`** mode). This layered approach ensures ongoing compliance throughout the resource lifecycle.

Benefits of Policy as Code

When implemented correctly, Policy as Code delivers three critical advantages for FinOps teams:

- **Consistency:** All resources follow the same rules, regardless of team or region
- **Scalability:** Policies apply uniformly across thousands of resources and accounts
- **Auditability:** Clear, machine-readable logs make compliance reporting faster and more reliable

These benefits go beyond cost management as they support security, regulatory compliance, and operational efficiency.

FinOps Tip: Treat tagging policies as living documentation of your cost governance model.

Well-structured policies serve as both enforcement mechanisms and reference guides. They clarify ownership models, define business contexts (for example, **`project`**, **`team`**), and make implicit assumptions explicit. This transparency helps onboard new teams and aligns stakeholders across finance, engineering, and compliance.

Common Pitfall: Overloading tagging with too many fields, leading to adoption fatigue.

While it is tempting to require 10+ tags per resource, excessive requirements are associated with a lesser degree of compliance. Teams prioritize functionality over bureaucratic norms, especially under increasing pressure to make important deliveries. Start with 3–5 essential tags (for example `owner`, `project`, `environment`, `cost-center`) and expand only when justified by the requirements of the business.

Large media organizations like Comcast and Netflix have shared valuable lessons about using Infrastructure as Code to strengthen cloud governance. One notable example involves a global media company that initially mandated twelve tags across its cloud estate. Adoption plateaued at about thirty-five percent, as teams struggled with the complexity. By simplifying the policy to five essential tags and enforcing them through Terraform, the company transformed its compliance rate—reaching over ninety percent within just three months.

Enforce with CI/CD Pipelines

Integrating tagging enforcement into CI/CD pipelines closes the loop between development and FinOps.

Example: Use Jenkins to block untagged Terraform deployments.

A Jenkins pipeline runs `Checkov` or `tflint` during the build stage to validate that all resources include required tags. If validation fails, the pipeline stops and no human approval can override it.

This automation ensures that cost accountability is not optional but embedded in the software delivery process.

FinOps Tip: Use immutable pipelines with automated policy gates to eliminate exceptions.

Allowing manual overrides for policy violations creates loopholes that erode governance. Instead, design pipelines where compliance is mandatory. If a deployment fails due to missing tags, the developer must fix the code and not merely request a bypass

Common Pitfall: Delaying policy feedback until late in the pipeline, increasing rework.

If tagging validation happens only during deployment (for example, in the "deploy" stage), developers may have to backtrack significant work. Instead, run policy checks early–during pull request reviews or local testing–so issues are caught immediately. Tools like pre-commit hooks or IDE integrations help surface problems before they enter the pipeline.

Case Study: Retail Tagging Overhaul

Challenge: A global retailer had 40% of its cloud resources untagged, resulting in $500K/year in unallocated costs. Finance couldn't assign spend to departments, and engineering spent hours tracing orphaned resources.

Solution:

- **Terraform:** Enforced mandatory tags for all new resources
- **Cloud Custodian:** Retroactively tagged legacy systems based on naming conventions, resource types, and ownership signals

Result: Achieved 95% tagging compliance in 6 months and saved $300K annually through better cost allocation and waste identification

FinOps Tip: Combine preventive and corrective strategies for full tagging coverage. Use Policy as Code for greenfield (new) resources and automated remediation tools like Cloud Custodian for brownfield (existing) environments. This dual approach ensures no part of your estate is left in the dark

Common Pitfall: Focusing only on new resources while ignoring legacy debt. Organizations often celebrate high compliance on new deployments while overlooking thousands of untagged legacy resources. These become long-term liabilities–hard to attribute, risky to delete, and costly to maintain. Prioritize a clean-up plan with tools that can infer tags based on context (for example, naming patterns, VPC membership, IAM roles)

Cloud Custodian: Beyond Basic Tagging

While Terraform prevents future tagging gaps, Cloud Custodian addresses the past. This open-source tool allows FinOps teams to automate tagging, monitoring, and remediation across multi-cloud environments.

Advanced Use Cases:

- **Conditional Tagging:** Automatically apply `env=prod` only to resources with >4 vCPUs
- **Multi-Resource Tagging:** Tag all resources within a VPC (EC2, S3, RDS) when one is tagged
- **Auto-Remediation:** Shut down untagged EC2 instances after 7 days of inactivity

FinOps Tip: Use Cloud Custodian to enforce tagging hygiene across multi-cloud and hybrid environments. Its declarative YAML-based policies make it easy to define complex logic once and deploy everywhere.

For example, an advanced use case that filter for resources missing EITHER Environment OR Owner tag.

The automated enforcement policy in the **yaml** file below scans EC2 instances for missing Environment or Owner tags, applies **ComplianceStatus** tagging to non-compliant resources, and alerts the CloudOps team – maintaining consistent tagging hygiene across all environments.

```
policies:
- name: enforce-required-tags
  resource: aws.ec2
  filters:
    - or:
      - "tag:Environment": absent
      - "tag:Owner": absent
  actions:
    - type: tag
      key: ComplianceStatus
      value: MissingRequiredTags
    - type: notify
      template: default
      subject: "Tagging Policy Violation Detected"
      to:
        - CloudOpsTeam@eava.com
```

***Figure** 7.3: Advanced Use Case of Cloud Custodian*

The policy will:

- Target AWS EC2 instances
- Filter for instances missing required tags
- Tag non-compliant resources with "**ComplianceStatus: MissingRequiredTags**"
- Send email notifications to the **CloudOps** team

Common Pitfall: Using auto-tagging without stakeholder communication, leading to confusion. Automatically applying tags—especially ownership tags—can create friction if teams are not informed. For example, tagging a resource with **Owner: Finance** when the finance team didn't request it may lead to unexpected cost allocation disputes. Always pair automation with clear communication, ownership workflows, and escalation paths

By embedding FinOps Tips and Common Pitfalls throughout this section, we reinforce exam-critical concepts such as shift-left governance, automation at scale, and compliance lifecycle management, while grounding them in practical, real-world scenarios. This

structure not only supports certification readiness but also drives operational excellence in FinOps practice.

Cost-Anomaly Detection with Cloud Custodian

Cloud Custodian is a versatile open-source tool designed to help organizations manage and optimize their cloud resources effectively. Beyond its core capabilities in governance, security, and compliance, Cloud Custodian can also be used for cost optimization by detecting anomalies in spending patterns. By leveraging policies that monitor resource usage and costs, organizations can proactively identify unexpected spikes or inefficiencies before they lead to significant financial impacts.

The following example demonstrates how Cloud Custodian can be configured to detect cost anomalies in Amazon S3 buckets and notify stakeholders via Slack when costs exceed predefined thresholds. This approach ensures that teams are alerted in real-time to potential issues, enabling prompt action to mitigate unnecessary expenses.

Cloud Custodian Cost Spike Alert

Cloud Custodian isn't just for enforcing tagging or compliance – it can also help detect and respond to unexpected cost spikes across your cloud environments. By defining policies that monitor spending trends, you can automatically trigger alerts or even mitigation actions when usage or cost exceeds normal thresholds.

The cost guardrail below monitors daily EC2 spending and triggers instant alerts upon crossing the $500 threshold, allowing FinOps teams to quickly address cost anomalies from misconfigured workloads or unexpected scaling before they become major budget concerns.

```yaml
policies:
  - name: detect-cost-spike
    resource: aws.ec2
    description: "Alert when daily EC2 spend exceeds normal thresholds."
    filters:
      - type: metrics
        name: EstimatedCharges
        namespace: AWS/Billing
        statistics: Average
        days: 1
        op: greater-than
        value: 500
    actions:
      - type: notify
        template: default
        subject: "⚠ Cost Spike Detected in EC2"
        to:
          - FinOpsTeam@ava.com
```

Figure 7.4: *Detecting Anomalies in S3 Costs with Cloud Custodian*

This policy:

- Monitors AWS Billing metrics for EC2 **`EstimatedCharges`**
- Triggers an alert to the FinOps team when daily average exceeds $500
- Helps quickly identify and address unexpected cost increases
- Enables rapid response to cost anomalies before they escalate

Case Study: Gaming Company Saves $80k/Month

- **Anomaly:** A misconfigured Lambda function invoked 10M times/hour
- **Detection:** CloudWatch Metrics + Cloud Custodian alerted within 15 minutes
- **Resolution:** Fixed code, capped concurrency, saved $80k

Retroactive Tagging with Ansible: Cleaning Up Legacy Tag Debt

Legacy cloud environments often suffer from tag debt, which refers to a backlog of untagged or inconsistently tagged resources that undermine cost visibility and accountability. Manual cleanup is slow, error-prone, and unsustainable. Automation offers a scalable solution to this problem.

A gaming studio reduced its tag debt by 80% using Ansible playbooks to auto-tag legacy AWS EC2 instances based on usage patterns. By analyzing instance configurations and application roles, they applied meaningful tags such as **`Application=GameServer`** and **`Environment=Production`**—without requiring manual input.

This effort saved hundreds of hours of labor and dramatically improved cost allocation accuracy across teams.

FinOps Tip: Use automation tools like Ansible, Cloud Custodian, or Terraform to infer and apply tags based on resource attributes and usage patterns. Retroactive tagging is not about guessing—it is about leveraging observable data (for example, AMI IDs, instance names, security groups, ports) to reconstruct context. For example:

- All instances using a specific database AMI → **`Application=MySQL`**, **`Tier=Data`**
- Instances named **`"gamesvr-*"`** → **`Application=GameServer`**, **`Environment=Production`**

This approach turns unstructured inventory into governed, cost-attributable assets.

Common Pitfall: Assuming all legacy resources can be tagged the same way and ignoring context and ownership. Automated tagging rules that are too broad can mislabel resources and create new inaccuracies. For example, applying **`Environment=Production`** to every instance with high CPU usage might incorrectly tag a dev batch job as production. Always validate tagging logic against a sample set and involve team leads to confirm accuracy before scaling.

One company auto-tagged 500 instances as "Finance" based on a naming pattern, only to discover later that the tag applied to a shared utility account used by multiple departments. The error led to incorrect chargebacks and required a full audit to correct it.

How the Gaming Studio Did It: A Step-by-Step Breakdown

The studio followed a structured workflow to tackle tag debt at scale:

1. **Inventory Discovery**

They used AWS CLI command to help create a comprehensive inventory of untagged and partially tagged resources by retrieving all EC2 instances with their associated metadata and tags, enabling systematic identification of compliance gaps across your environment. An example is shown below:

```
aws ec2 describe-instances --query 'Reservations[].Instances[].[InstanceId, Tags,
LaunchTime, ImageId, PrivateDnsName]'
```

***Figure* 7.5**: AWS CLI *Tag*

This command will output a formatted list showing:

- Instance ID
- Tags (for tag compliance checking)
- Launch Time
- Image ID (AMI)
- Private DNS Name

This is useful for auditing EC2 instances and verifying tag compliance across your AWS environment.

2. **Pattern Matching**

Analyzed instance configurations to identify application roles:

- Instances with **`port 27015`** open → likely game servers
- AMI ID **`ami-db10293`** → known database image
- Hostnames starting with **`"gs-"`** → game server fleet

3. **Tagging Automation**

Built Ansible playbooks to apply standardized tags:

```
- name: Tag game servers
  hosts: localhost
  tasks:
    - name: Apply GameServer tag
      aws_ec2_tag:
        region: us-east-1
        resource: "{{ item.InstanceId }}"
        tags:
          Application: GameServer
          Environment: Production
          Owner: games-team
      loop: "{{ ec2_instances }}"
      when: "'gamesvr' in item.PrivateDnsName"
```

***Figure 7.6**: Automating Tagging*

This playbook will:

- Iterate through a list of EC2 instances (**`ec2_instances`**)
- Identify instances with **`'gamesvr'`** in their Private DNS name
- Apply standardized tags (**`Application`**, **`Environment`**, **`Owner`**) to those game servers
- Help maintain consistent tagging for game server resources in the AWS environment

FinOps Tip: Treat retroactive tagging as a data enrichment process. Start with high-impact, easily identifiable resources first. Do not forget to focus on:

- Resources with high spend
- Instances in production environments
- Systems tied to major business units

This prioritization delivers quick wins and builds momentum for broader cleanup. For example, tagging just the top 20% of cost-generating untagged instances can restore visibility into 80% of unallocated spend.

Common Pitfall: Running bulk tagging without dry runs or rollback plans. A poorly tested playbook can accidentally overwrite existing tags or mislabel critical systems. Always remember to:

- Run a dry-run mode to preview changes
- Backup current tags before modification

- Use version-controlled playbooks with peer review

One organization accidentally removed **`compliance=HIPAA`** tags from 50 medical data instances during a bulk update, triggering a compliance review and delaying a product launch.

Retroactive Tagging at Scale: Integrating with Cloud-Native Tools

While Ansible works well for structured, cross-account automation, cloud-native tools like AWS Resource Groups and Cloud Custodian offer even greater scalability for tagging at enterprise levels.

Workflow for Large-Scale Retroactive Tagging:

1. **Inventory Untagged Resources**

Use AWS Resource Groups or Tag Editor to find all resources with specific tags:

```
aws resourcegroupstaggingapi get-resources --tag-filters Key=Environment,
Values=Production --resources-per-page 10
```

***Figure 7.7**: Query Resources by Tag Filter*

This command will:

- Query AWS resources using the Resource Groups Tagging API
- Filter for resources with the **`Environment=Production`** tag
- Return results in pages of 10 resources at a time
- Help identify and audit resources based on specific tag criteria

2. **Deploy Cloud Custodian policies to auto-tag based on patterns**

Lifecycle Management: Optimizing Resources from Creation to Retirement

Effective lifecycle management ensures that cloud resources are created, scaled, and terminated in alignment with actual business needs. Without oversight, resources often remain active long after their purpose has ended, driving up costs and increasing operational complexity. Automation adds a critical safety net, enabling teams to scale confidently while preventing runaway spending.

By integrating cost controls into operational workflows, organizations shift from reactive cost cleanup to proactive financial governance.

FinOps Tip: Automate scaling *and* cost monitoring together to maintain performance without budget overruns. Scaling infrastructure to meet demand is essential, but without cost visibility, it can lead to unexpected and escalating bills. Pairing Auto Scaling Groups with real-time cost alerts ensures that performance and financial outcomes are balanced. This dual-control model is especially critical during high-traffic events like product launches or seasonal peaks.

Common Pitfall: Automating scale-up without automating cost awareness leads to "scaling debt." Teams often focus on technical scalability (for example, handling traffic spikes) but neglect financial scalability.

For example, an Auto Scaling Group may launch dozens of EC2 instances during a marketing campaign, but if no one monitors the associated cost trajectory, the final bill could be 3x the forecast. This disconnect between engineering and finance undermines trust and can lead to restrictive budget policies in the future.

One company experienced a $200,000 overspend during a holiday sale because their scaling logic responded perfectly to traffic, but no one was alerted until the monthly bill arrived. By then, the cost was irreversible.

Auto-Scaling with Alerts: Staying in Budget During Peak Demand

An e-commerce team configured AWS Auto Scaling Groups to handle Black Friday traffic but added a Lambda function to alert them if costs exceeded a 3-hour forecast. This combination of automation and real-time monitoring allowed them to scale dynamically while staying within budget.

Here is how it worked:

- **Auto Scaling Configuration:** Auto Scaling Groups adjusted EC2 instance counts based on CPU utilization
- **Cost Monitoring:** A Lambda function queried the AWS Cost Explorer API every 15 minutes to project near-term spend
- **Alerts:** If projected costs exceeded a predefined threshold, a Slack notification was sent to the on-call team

FinOps Tip: Use short-interval cost forecasting (for example hourly or 3-hour windows) during high-risk periods to enable rapid intervention. Traditional monthly forecasting is not enough during volatile events. Short-term projections–powered by real-time APIs–allow FinOps teams to detect anomalies early and adjust scaling policies before costs spiral. This is part of continuous cost observability, a core FinOps practice.

Common Pitfall: Relying solely on infrastructure metrics (like CPU) without correlating them to cost impact. It is easy to optimize for performance (for example keeping CPU under 70%), but that does not guarantee cost efficiency. A low-CPU instance might still be oversized or underutilized. Always pair performance automation with cost intelligence. For example, use AWS Compute Optimizer alongside Auto Scaling to ensure instances are both performant *and* right-sized.

In one such case, a media company scaled up hundreds of instances for a live stream, but many ran at less than 10% utilization. Since they weren't monitoring cost-per-function, they wasted over $50,000 on over-provisioned capacity.

Expiration Policies with a Human Touch: Automation with Accountability

Automation is not equal to autocracy. Netflix's Janitor Monkey, an open-source tool, exemplifies the balance between efficiency and ownership. It identifies and terminates unused resources, but only after notifying the owner and granting time to respond.

For example: An EC2 instance idle for 30 days triggers a Slack message to its owner: *"The EC2 instance i-1234567890abcdef0 has been idle for 30 days. It will be terminated in 7 days unless you respond to this message."*

If no response is received, the resource is automatically decommissioned.

FinOps Tip: Implement graceful decommissioning workflows that notify owners before deletion to preserve trust and accountability. Automated cleanup is powerful, but abrupt deletions can damage team morale and create operational risk. A phased approach—**`detect → notify → confirm → terminate`**—ensures that automation supports, rather than overrides, human judgment. This fosters a culture of ownership and reduces resistance to FinOps initiatives

Common Pitfall: Fully automated cleanup without ownership signals leads to accidental deletions and team frustration. Imagine that a data science team is running a long-running experiment on a low-utilization instance. If an automated script deletes it based solely on CPU usage, weeks of work could be lost. Without clear ownership tagging or business context, automation becomes a liability

Always ensure:

- Resources have accurate **`owner`** and **`project`** tags
- Notification channels (for example, Slack, email) are reliable
- There is an easy way to **`"opt out"`** or extend lifecycle (for example, via a comment or label)

One tech firm automated resource deletion without notifications and accidentally terminated a CEO's sandbox environment before a board demo. The incident delayed FinOps adoption by months due to eroded trust.

Best Practices for Lifecycle Automation

To maximize cost efficiency while minimizing risk, combine technical automation with human-centered design:

1. **Tag First, Automate Later:** Ensure all resources have ownership and purpose metadata before applying lifecycle policies
2. **Use Time-Based Tiers**: Apply increasingly aggressive actions over time (for example, `warn at 14 days idle → stop at 30 days → terminate at 60 days`)
3. **Integrate with Incident Tools:** Route cleanup alerts into existing workflows (for example, Jira, PagerDuty) to reduce noise and improve response rates
4. **Measure Impact:** Track savings from terminated resources and share wins across teams to build FinOps momentum

FinOps Tip: Treat lifecycle automation as an iterative process—start small, measure results, and expand gradually. Begin with non-critical environments (for example, dev/test), then scale to production. This reduces risk and allows teams to refine policies based on feedback. Celebrate early wins (for example, "We saved $10K by retiring 200 idle resources") to build cross-functional support.

Common Pitfall: One-size-fits-all policies ignore workload diversity and business context.

Not all low-utilization resources are wasted. A database might have low CPU but high I/O or store critical data. A staging environment might be used once a quarter. Avoid rigid thresholds. Instead, use context-aware policies that consider resource type, tags, and historical usage patterns.

For example:

Only target EC2 instances in dev environment with <5% CPU for 30 days

By embedding FinOps Tips and Common Pitfalls throughout this section, we align lifecycle management practices with exam-critical themes such as automation with guardrails, cross-functional collaboration, and continuous cost optimization. These insights not only prepare learners for certification but also equip them to implement sustainable, trusted FinOps programs in real organizations.

Expiration Policies with a Human Touch

Netflix's open-source tool **Janitor Monkey** illustrates how automation can drive cost efficiency without losing human oversight. Built as part of the Simian Army suite, Janitor Monkey identifies and schedules the cleanup of **unused or idle cloud resources**, a common source of waste in large-scale environments.

However, instead of immediately deleting idle assets, the tool introduces a **human approval loop**. For instance, if an **EC2 instance** has been idle for 30 days, Janitor Monkey sends a **Slack notification** to the owner:

> *"The EC2 instance i-1234567890abcdef0 has been idle for 30 days. It will be terminated in 7 days unless you respond to this message."*

This approach gives engineers a chance to review their workloads and justify resource retention before termination. If no action is taken, the instance is automatically decommissioned – reducing unnecessary spend and freeing up budget for higher-value initiatives.

By embedding communication and accountability into cost-control automation, Netflix demonstrates a key FinOps principle: **effective cost management isn't just about automation – it is about aligning financial responsibility with engineering ownership.**

AWS Auto Scaling Group (ASG) Configuration: One of the most practical ways to apply FinOps principles at the infrastructure layer is through AWS Auto Scaling Groups (ASGs). Configurations like the following ensure that compute resources automatically scale with demand – preventing over-provisioning and aligning cloud spend with real usage.

```
{
  "AutoScalingGroupName": "prod-web-servers",
  "MinSize": 2,
  "MaxSize": 10,
  "DesiredCapacity": 4,
  "TargetTrackingConfigurations": [
    {
      "PredefinedMetricSpecification": {
        "PredefinedMetricType": "ASGAverageCPUUtilization"
      },
      "TargetValue": 60.0
    }
  ]
}
```

Figure 7.8: *Auto Scaling Group Configuration*

This configuration defines a production Auto Scaling Group that keeps at least two instances running and can grow up to ten as demand increases. The target tracking policy maintains an average CPU utilization of 60%, meaning instances are only added when utilization exceeds that threshold and removed when it drops.

The configuration ensures cost-efficient scaling by maintaining optimal resource utilization while meeting performance requirements.

From a **FinOps perspective**, this setup exemplifies **dynamic right-sizing** – ensuring teams pay only for the compute power they actually need. By letting performance metrics drive scaling decisions, organizations strike a balance between cost control and reliability, embodying the FinOps goal of achieving **maximum business value per dollar spent**.

Why Automation Transforms Tagging

Automation transforms tagging and resource management by addressing the limitations of manual processes. Human-driven tagging is often inconsistent, forgotten during rapid deployments, or applied incorrectly, leading to compliance gaps, cost allocation errors, and operational blind spots. Automation eliminates these risks by enforcing tagging policies at the point of resource creation, ensuring every instance, bucket, or container is properly labeled from the start.

By integrating tagging rules into deployment workflows and cloud governance tools such as Cloud Custodian, organizations achieve uniformity across environments, improve accountability, and enable downstream processes such as cost allocation, security monitoring, and asset inventory. Automated tagging turns metadata into a strategic asset, which is reliable, searchable, and actionable.

Comparison of Manual vs. Automated Cloud Resource Management Processes

This table highlights the key advantages of automation in cloud operations. While manual processes are slow, error-prone, and lack visibility, automated approaches powered by tools like Cloud Custodian deliver efficiency, accuracy, and real-time compliance. Automation also enhances cost management by enabling consistent policy enforcement and proactive identification of waste, leading to more transparent, scalable, and financially sound cloud environments.

Aspect	**Manual Process**	**Automated Process**
Efficiency	Time-consuming and error-prone	Fast, consistent, and scalable
Accuracy	Prone to human error	Enforces rules programmatically
Visibility	Limited insights into resource usage	Provides clear metadata for better tracking

Compliance	High risk of non-compliance	Ensures adherence to regulatory standards
Cost Management	Difficult to identify and eliminate waste	Enables proactive cost optimization

Table 7.1: *Manual vs. Automated Cloud Resource Management*

This table contrasts the operational characteristics of manual processes against automated systems, highlighting how automation directly enables the core principles of the Operate phase.

By automating tagging and lifecycle management, organizations can achieve greater efficiency, accountability, and cost savings. Whether through Policy-As-Code tools such as Terraform or lifecycle management tools such as Janitor Monkey, automation ensures that cloud resources are always aligned with business priorities.

Why Forecasting Matters: A Cautionary Tale

In cloud financial management, **forecasting isn't just a budgeting exercise – it is a survival skill.** When organizations fail to anticipate usage patterns or factors in upcoming projects, cloud costs can surge unexpectedly, often without corresponding business value. Industry reports consistently identify poor forecasting as one of the top causes of cloud overspend. According to the **Flexera 2024 State of the Cloud Report**, over **82% of enterprises** cite "managing cloud spend" as their biggest challenge, with unplanned cost spikes being a recurring theme.

A notable example comes from a mid-sized **e-commerce company** featured in a **FinOps Foundation case study**. During a major product launch, the business experienced a sudden surge in traffic that triggered large-scale auto-scaling events across multiple regions. The engineering team celebrated the system's reliability – until the next month's bill arrived. Cloud costs had increased by **over 350%** because no one had forecasted the cost impact of scaling, data egress, and storage growth.

The company's FinOps team later implemented **usage forecasting models** using historical metrics from AWS Cost Explorer and business growth projections. By integrating forecasts into their CI/CD planning cycle, they improved budget predictability and secured **Savings Plans** in advance – reducing their monthly compute cost by **28%**.

This real-world scenario highlights a fundamental FinOps principle:

> **You cannot optimize what you do not forecast.**

Forecasting connects business intent with engineering activity – turning reactive cost management into proactive financial planning.

Forecasting: Turning Data into Financial Foresight

In 2022, a SaaS company burned through $500,000 in cloud credits due to unchecked Kubernetes cluster scaling. Their biggest mistake was relying on a gut feeling instead of data-driven forecasting. This costly incident underscores a critical principle in modern FinOps: accurate forecasting is not just helpful; it is essential for survival in dynamic cloud environments.

Forecasting transforms historical usage and cost data into actionable insights, enabling organizations to anticipate spending trends, allocate budgets with confidence, and avoid billing surprises. For businesses with fluctuating workloads, such as e-commerce platforms during Black Friday or media companies launching viral content, forecasting is not optional. Without it, teams risk either overspending on idle resources or under-provisioning during peak demand, leading to degraded performance and poor customer experiences.

Machine Learning: The Engine behind Modern Forecasting

Advanced forecasting now leverages Machine Learning (ML) models to detect complex usage patterns and seasonality. Two widely used approaches in this domain are Facebook's Prophet and Long Short-Term Memory (LSTM) networks. Each has strengths depending on data volume, infrastructure complexity, and operational needs that are mentioned as follows:

Feature	Prophet	LSTM
Best For	Structured, time-series data with clear seasonality	High-dimensional, non-linear patterns (for example microservices)
Data Requirements	Moderate (months of daily data)	High (large, granular datasets)
Training Complexity	Low – easy to implement and interpret	High – requires ML expertise and tuning
Scalability	Suitable for individual services or teams	Ideal for enterprise-wide forecasting
Accuracy (Real-World)	~92–95% during stable periods	~94–97% in volatile environments (for example Q4 spikes)
Use Case Example	Predicting monthly S3 and EC2 spend for budgeting	Forecasting Kubernetes pod scaling costs during product launches

Table 7.2: *Machine Learning Models for Cloud Cost Forecasting*

This table compares two prominent ML approaches, highlighting their ideal use cases, requirements, and practical performance for predicting cloud spend.

The following example effectively illustrates the importance of advanced forecasting:

A global e-commerce platform achieved 95% accuracy in Q4 spend forecasting using Prophet, allowing them to lock in Reserved Instances six months in advance and reduce compute costs by 38%. Meanwhile, a streaming service used LSTM models to predict traffic surges during content drops, dynamically scaling infrastructure while staying within budget.

Aligning Forecasting with Cost Optimization

The true power of forecasting emerges when integrated with cost-saving commitments like Reserved Instances (RIs) or Savings Plans. Accurate predictions allow organizations to:

- **Right-size commitments:** Purchase RIs based on forecasted utilization, not guesswork
- **Avoid waste:** Prevent over-committing during anticipated demand drops
- **Maximize discounts:** Lock in pricing during low-usage periods for high-growth phases

Without alignment between forecasting and procurement strategy, even the most accurate models fail to deliver ROI. Leading FinOps teams treat forecasting as a continuous feedback loop, refines models with actual spend data, and adjusts reservations quarterly.

In short, forecasting powered by machine learning turns reactive cost management into proactive financial planning and shapes the future instead of merely predicting it.

Building a Forecasting Script: Step-by-Step

Forecasting cloud spend doesn't require advanced data science : a simple, automated script can give FinOps teams the clarity they need to plan ahead. The process begins by **extracting historical cost data** from your cloud provider's billing APIs (such as AWS Cost Explorer or Azure Cost Management). Once collected, the data is **cleaned and aggregated** to show daily or weekly spend patterns.

Next, apply a **lightweight forecasting model** like Facebook Prophet or exponential smoothing to project the next 30 days of costs based on past usage trends. The output can then be visualized in a simple chart, helping teams spot rising costs or seasonal spikes before they happen.

Finally, automate the script to run regularly – for example, every month – and share the results with engineering and finance through dashboards or Slack updates.

By turning historical billing data into forward-looking insight, organizations can move from reactive cost reviews to **proactive cloud financial planning** – a foundational FinOps capability.

Scenario Modeling: What-If Analysis

Scenario modeling helps assess the financial impact of changes. For example, a media company modeled the cost of migrating 500TB of data to AWS Glacier vs. Google Coldline, factoring in retrieval fees. This analysis revealed that AWS Glacier was more cost-effective for long-term storage, while Google Coldline offered better pricing for frequent access.

Predictive Cost Modeling with Machine Learning

Once you have reliable forecasting in place, the next FinOps frontier is prediction – using machine learning to anticipate cloud costs based on usage drivers, seasonality, and business activity. Predictive cost modeling helps organizations move beyond trend extrapolation to truly **data-driven forecasting**.

A typical workflow begins by gathering historical cost and usage data from billing APIs or data warehouses such as AWS CUR or Azure Cost Management exports. These datasets are then enriched with contextual signals – like deployment schedules, user growth, or feature releases – to capture business-driven cost patterns.

Next, a regression or time-series model (for example, **Facebook Prophet**, **XGBoost**, or **AutoML Forecast**) is trained to predict future spend. The model learns relationships between resource consumption, pricing changes, and scaling events, generating forecasts with confidence intervals that finance teams can rely on.

Once validated, the model can run automatically – predicting costs daily or weekly – and publish insights to dashboards or Slack channels. Over time, this approach helps FinOps teams detect anomalies early, plan capacity more accurately, and **align engineering spend with business demand**.

Detecting Anomalies Before They Escalate

Machine learning algorithms excel at identifying anomalies. A streaming service flagged a misconfigured Lambda function that racked up $20k in unintended API calls using clustering algorithms. By detecting unusual usage patterns early, they avoided further escalation of costs.

Time-Series Forecasting in Action

Time-series models capture complex usage patterns, enabling proactive cost management. For example:

Data Prep: Engineer features such as **"month-end rush"** or **"holiday season"** to capture business cycles.

Model Selection:

- **Prophet:** Best for datasets with strong seasonality (for example, retail sales cycles).
- **LSTM:** Ideal for capturing patterns in high-frequency data (for example, real-time gaming traffic).

Tool Demo: Azure Cost Management's ML-powered recommendations helped a logistics firm save 18% by switching 300 VMs to reserved instances

ML-Driven Forecasting with Prophet

Machine learning simplifies forecasting when paired with the right tools – and **Facebook's Prophet** stands out for its ability to model complex, seasonally driven cloud spending patterns with minimal tuning.

```
from prophet import Prophet
import pandas as pd

# Load historical cost data
df = pd.read_csv('cloud_costs.csv')
df['ds'] = pd.to_datetime(df['date'])
df['y'] = df['cost']

# Train model
model = Prophet(yearly_seasonality=True, weekly_seasonality=True)
model.fit(df)

# Predict next quarter
future = model.make_future_dataframe(periods=90)
forecast = model.predict(future)

# Plot results
fig = model.plot(forecast)
```

***Figure 7.9**: Cloud Cost Forecasting with Facebook Prophet*

This code demonstrates how to use Facebook Prophet for predicting cloud costs by analyzing historical spending patterns and seasonal trends to generate accurate 90-day forecasts.

Machine learning simplifies forecasting when paired with the right tools – and Facebook's Prophet stands out for its ability to model complex, seasonally driven cloud spending patterns with minimal tuning. This code demonstrates how to use Facebook Prophet for predicting cloud costs by analyzing historical spending patterns and seasonal trends to generate accurate 90-day forecasts.

Overcoming ML Challenges

While machine learning can unlock powerful insights in cloud cost forecasting, it's not without pitfalls. Models can drift over time, miss unexpected business events, or overfit to past patterns that no longer apply. Common challenges include **data quality issues**, sudden usage spikes, or a lack of alignment between technical modeling and financial reality.

A FinTech team's model, for instance, failed because it didn't account for a major new product launch – leading to significant forecast errors. They now **retrain models quarterly** and **involve finance teams in feature selection** to ensure new business drivers are captured early.

This experience underscores that **predictive modeling in FinOps isn't just about technology – it's about collaboration, feedback, and continuous improvement**.

Real-World Use Cases

Automating Governance at a Retail Giant

Challenge: 40% of resources lacked cost center tags, causing internal disputes **Solution:** A Terraform pipeline enforced tags at provisioning, while a Slack bot reminded teams to tag legacy resources.

Result: 95% tagging compliance within 6 months.

ML-Driven Savings in Ad Tech.

Problem: Unpredictable ad traffic led to overspending on AWS Spot Instances **Solution:** A custom ML model predicted traffic spikes, reducing interruptions by 35%.

Driving FinOps with Automation and Culture

Automation succeeds when paired with cultural shifts: One effective practice is hosting a **"Cost Clinic"** where engineers present resource plans to finance teams for feedback. This fosters collaboration, shared accountability, and smarter decision-making.

Celebrate Wins: A DevOps team boosted participation by **60%** by launching a **"Cost Efficiency Leaderboard"** to gamify savings. Recognizing and rewarding progress reinforces positive behaviors and encourages continuous improvement.

Why Automation Matters

Automation is not about replacing people, but about **empowering them to focus on high-impact work.** By blending code, data, and collaboration, FinOps becomes a superpower for your organization.

As cloud environments grow more complex, teams that embrace automation will thrive. Automation streamlines processes, reduces errors, and delivers real-time insights, helping organizations make faster, more informed decisions.

Manual vs. Automated Tagging: Comparison Table

While both manual and automated approaches aim to achieve resource accountability, the method an organization chooses fundamentally dictates the strategy's scalability, accuracy, and overall return on investment, with automated enforcement consistently proving superior in maintaining compliance at scale while reducing operational overhead.

Category	Manual Tagging	Automated Tagging
Efficiency	Time-consuming, error-prone	Fast, consistent, scalable
Accuracy	Prone to human error	Programmatically enforced rules
Visibility	Limited insights	Clear metadata for tracking
Compliance	High risk of non-compliance	Ensures adherence to standards
Cost Mgmt	Hard to spot waste	Enables proactive optimization

Table 7.3: *Manual vs. Automated Tagging Comparison*

This table contrasts the operational impact of manual tagging processes against automated enforcement, demonstrating how automation is critical for achieving reliable cost allocation and governance.

Forecasting Flow Diagram

Figure 7.10 below illustrates the end-to-end process of automated anomaly detection in financial operations. It begins with **data collection**, where cost and usage metrics are aggregated from multiple cloud sources. The next phase, **analysis**, processes this data to identify trends and performance baselines. During **anomaly detection**, the system applies statistical or machine learning models to flag deviations from expected patterns. Finally, the **alerting** stage notifies stakeholders through dashboards or automated messages, enabling timely action to prevent budget overruns or resource misallocations.

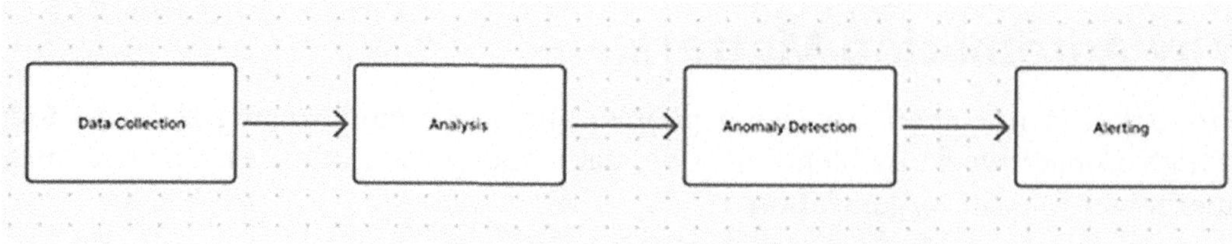

***Figure* 7.10**: *Anomaly Detection Workflow in FinOps*

Lifecycle Automation Triggers Diagram

Depicts automation at each stage of a cloud resource's lifecycle—**creation, scaling, monitoring, termination**—ensuring consistency and compliance with integrations (for example, Cloud Custodian + AWS Cost Explorer) predicting spend and triggering timely actions.

Anomaly Detection Loop

Figure 7.11 illustrates the **Anomaly Detection Loop**, a continuous feedback system central to FinOps automation. The loop begins with **monitoring**, where cloud usage and spend data are tracked in real time. When deviations occur, the system **detects anomalies** and **triggers alerts** to notify engineers or financial teams. These teams then take **corrective action**—such as tuning autoscaling policies, modifying budgets, or shutting down idle resources. Finally, they **review performance** to validate outcomes and improve detection accuracy. This cyclical process ensures that cost optimization remains **dynamic, data-driven,** and **self-correcting** over time.

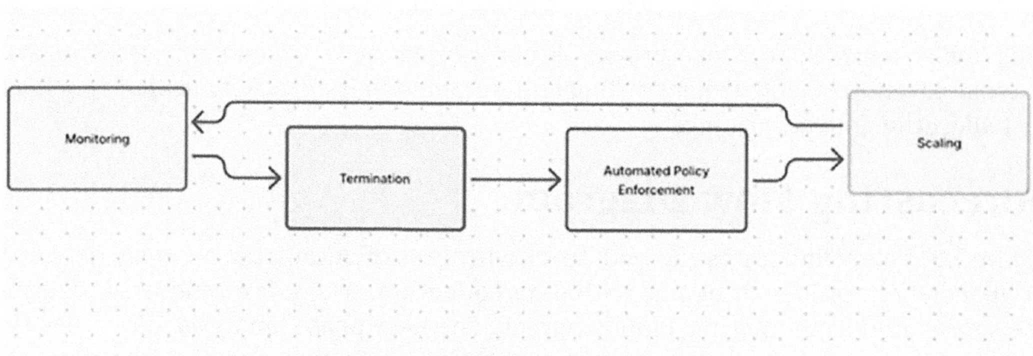

***Figure* 7.11**: *Anomaly Detection Loop*

A circular feedback loop: **`monitor → detect anomalies → trigger alerts → corrective action → review performance.`** Reinforces automation as an ongoing process

Tool Summary Table

In the FinOps (Cloud Financial Management) lifecycle – covering *inform, optimize, and operate* phases – various tools help organizations gain visibility into cloud spending, enforce governance, automate cost controls, and improve financial accountability. The following table summarizes key tools used across Azure, AWS, and multi-cloud environments that enable FinOps excellence.

Tool	**Category**	**Strengths**
AWS Budgets	Financial Monitoring and Alerts	Simple setup for custom spend thresholds and basic alerting via email/SNS.
AWS Cost Explorer	Cost Visualization and Reporting	Intuitive interface for visualizing and analyzing historical AWS cost and usage.
Azure Cost Management	Cost Visualization and Reporting	Native reporting and budgeting for Azure environments, with cost analysis views.
CloudHealth by VMware	Centralized Management Platform	Robust policy engine and comprehensive reporting for multi-cloud environments (AWS, Azure, GCP).
Cloud Custodian	Governance and Automation	Open-source, powerful policy-as-code tool for automated compliance and resource management.
Terraform	Infrastructure as Code (IaC)	Enforces tagging and resource configuration at deployment, preventing untagged resources.
Apptio Cloudability	Centralized Management Platform	Strong business mapping and allocation features for large enterprises.
Flexera One	Centralized Management Platform	Combines cloud cost optimization with SaaS and vendor management capabilities. g

Table 7.4: *FinOps Tool Comparison by Platform and Capability*

Conclusion

Treat your cloud like a **living ecosystem, not a static spreadsheet.** With the right tools and culture, it can become a **self-healing, cost-optimized system** that fuels innovation.

By investing in automation (Cloud Custodian, Terraform, Ansible, and others), your teams shift from firefighting to strategy by driving growth, efficiency, and resilience in the cloud. In the next chapter, we will know how to prepare for the certification exam.

Key Terms

- **FinOps (Financial Operations):** A cultural and operational practice that brings together finance, engineering, and business teams to manage cloud costs effectively, enabling data-driven decisions and accountability
- **Automation in FinOps:** The use of tools and scripts to enforce policies, optimize resources, and provide real-time insights without manual intervention, improving efficiency and accuracy in cloud cost management
- **Tagging:** The process of assigning metadata (for example, owner, project, environment) to cloud resources to enable cost allocation, governance, and visibility
- **Policy as Code:** A method of defining governance rules (for example, tagging, security) in code format, enabling automated enforcement during infrastructure provisioning
- **Lifecycle Management:** The practice of managing cloud resources from creation to retirement, including scaling, right-sizing, and decommissioning to avoid waste
- **Cost Anomaly Detection:** Identifying unexpected spikes in cloud spending using monitoring tools and machine learning to trigger alerts and prevent budget overruns
- **Forecasting:** Predicting future cloud costs using historical data, business context, and machine learning models to guide budgeting and procurement.
- **Reserved Instances (RIs) / Savings Plans:** Commitment-based pricing models offered by cloud providers that reduce costs when usage is predictable and aligned with forecasts
- **Prophet:** An open-source time-series forecasting tool developed by Meta (formerly Facebook), ideal for data with strong seasonality and trend patterns

- **LSTM (Long Short-Term Memory):** A type of Recurrent Neural Network (RNN) used in machine learning for forecasting complex, non-linear usage patterns in dynamic environments
- **Configuration Drift:** When deployed infrastructure deviates from its intended state (for example, manually added untagged resources), leading to compliance and cost risks
- **CI/CD Pipeline Enforcement:** Integrating policy checks (for example, tagging compliance) into continuous integration and delivery workflows to block non-compliant deployments
- **Retroactive Tagging:** Applying tags to existing (legacy) cloud resources using automation tools to clean up "tag debt" and improve cost visibility.
- **Graceful Decommissioning:** Automatically identifying idle resources but notifying owners before deletion, allowing for justification or extension—balancing automation with accountability
- **Shift-Left Governance:** Embedding compliance and cost controls early in the development lifecycle (for example, at deployment time) rather than fixing issues later

Points to Remember

- Automation is not about replacing people—it is about empowering them to focus on innovation by eliminating repetitive, error-prone tasks.
- Tagging is the foundation of cost visibility; without consistent, automated tagging, cost allocation and accountability are nearly impossible.
- Policy as Code (for example, using Terraform, AWS Config, or OPA) ensures that governance is consistent, scalable, and auditable.
- Manual tagging fails at scale—automation must be applied at deployment time and continuously monitored to prevent drift.
- Lifecycle management prevents "zombie" resources—idle VMs, orphaned disks, and forgotten environments that waste money.
- Forecasting bridges finance and engineering, turning historical data into actionable budgets, and procurement strategies.
- Machine learning models like Prophet and LSTM enhance forecasting accuracy, especially during volatile periods like product launches or holiday seasons.
- Align forecasting with Reserved Instances or Savings Plans to maximize discounts and avoid over-commitment.

- Anomaly detection tools like Cloud Custodian can catch cost spikes in real time–for example, a misconfigured Lambda function–saving tens of thousands of dollars.
- Automation without communication leads to distrust–tools like Netflix's Janitor Monkey succeed because they notify owners before taking action.
- Start small, measure impact, and scale–begin automation in dev environments, celebrate wins, and expand gradually.

Questions

1. Why is tagging considered the "cornerstone" of FinOps, and how does automation improve its effectiveness compared to manual processes?
2. Describe a scenario where poor forecasting led to a significant cloud cost overrun. How could machine learning have prevented it?
3. What are the risks of implementing fully automated resource deletion without human oversight? How can organizations balance automation with accountability?
4. Compare and contrast Prophet and LSTM for cloud cost forecasting. In what situations would you choose one over the other?
5. How can integrating tagging enforcement into CI/CD pipelines improve both compliance and team collaboration?
6. Explain the concept of "shift-left governance" in the context of FinOps. Provide an example of how it can prevent cost waste.
7. A company has thousands of untagged legacy resources. What steps would you take to clean up this "tag debt" using automation?
8. How does aligning forecasting with Reserved Instance purchases improve cost efficiency? What happens if forecasts are inaccurate?
9. Why is it important to treat the cloud as a "living ecosystem" rather than a static budget line item?
10. Discuss the cultural challenges of introducing automation in FinOps. How can teams overcome resistance from engineering or finance stakeholders?

Multiple Choice Questions

1. What is the primary goal of automation in FinOps?
    a. Replace finance teams with software
    b. Reduce cloud provider costs through negotiation
    c. Turn cost management into a competitive advantage
    d. Eliminate all human involvement in cloud operations
2. Which tool is commonly used to enforce tagging policies at deployment time using Infrastructure as Code (IaC)?
    a. Jenkins
    b. Terraform
    c. Grafana
    d. Tableau
3. What is the main benefit of using "Policy as Code" in cloud governance?
    a. It allows manual overrides for urgent deployments.
    b. It ensures consistent, scalable, and auditable enforcement of rules.
    c. It reduces the need for monitoring tools.
    d. It eliminates the need for forecasting.
4. Which forecasting model is best suited for datasets with strong seasonality, such as retail sales cycles?
    a. LSTM
    b. Prophet
    c. Linear Regression
    d. Decision Tree
5. What is a key risk of relying solely on historical spend data for forecasting?
    a. It is too accurate.
    b. It ignores business velocity and upcoming changes (for example product launches).

   c. It requires too much automation.
   d. It only works with AWS.
6. Which of the following best describes “graceful decommissioning”?
   a. Immediately deleting all idle resources
   b. Sending alerts only after deletion
   c. Notifying resource owners before termination and allowing opt-out
   d. Manually reviewing every resource monthly
7. What is “configuration drift” in cloud environments?
   a. When cloud providers change pricing
   b. When infrastructure changes outside of IaC templates, leading to non-compliance
   c. When forecasting models become inaccurate
   d. When teams use different tagging formats
8. Which tool is specifically designed for retroactive tagging and cost anomaly detection across multi-cloud environments?
   a. Ansible
   b. AWS Budgets
   c. Cloud Custodian
   d. Azure Monitor
9. Why is aligning forecasting with Reserved Instances important?
   a. To increase cloud spending
   b. To ensure over-provisioning
   c. To maximize discounts and avoid waste
   d. To eliminate the need for tagging

10. What is a major limitation of manual tagging in large-scale cloud environments?
    a. It is too fast.
    b. It is consistent across teams.
    c. It is time-consuming, error-prone, and unsustainable.
    d. It integrates well with CI/CD.

Answers

1. c
2. b
3. b
4. b
5. b
6. c
7. b
8. c
9. c
10. c

CHAPTER 8
Certification Preparation and Practice Questions

Introduction

Welcome to this chapter of your FinOps journey, where you will learn how to prepare for the certification exam! By now, you have gained a solid understanding of the principles, frameworks, and practices that define FinOps. This chapter is designed to help you consolidate your knowledge, identify weak areas, and prepare effectively for the FinOps certification exam. We will break down the syllabus, highlight common pitfalls, and provide realistic practice questions with detailed explanations to ensure that you are ready to succeed.

Structure

In this chapter, we will cover the following topics:

- A breakdown of all the sections of the certification exam
- Tips to avoid common mistakes
- Realistic practice tests with answers and explanations

Let us Dive in and Begin!

Automation is the engine of modern FinOps; but it is not limited to tools. It is also about culture, collaboration, and clarity. As cloud environments grow in scale and complexity, manual cost management becomes unsustainable. The solution to these challenges lies in a disciplined and automated approach grounded in shared ownership and data-driven decisions.

To help you master both the certification objectives and real-world applications of FinOps, we have distilled the most critical and recurring themes from this chapter into a concise set of FinOps Golden Rules, which are principles that appear across domains and underpin a successful automation strategy.

FinOps Golden Rules: 10 Principles to Live By

Achieving cloud cost efficiency requires more than just periodic reviews or isolated efforts; it demands a cultural shift supported by a disciplined operational framework. FinOps provides this structure, unifying technology, finance, and business teams around a shared goal of maximizing cloud value. The journey from reactive cost management to proactive optimization is guided by a set of foundational tenets. These principles are designed to instill accountability, drive intelligent automation, and align every cloud dollar with tangible business outcomes. The following ten rules serve as essential pillars for any organization committed to building a sustainable and cost-conscious cloud operating model.

S. No.	Principle	Why It Matters
1.	Rightsizing Comes before Commitments	Never purchase Reserved Instances or Savings Plans without first optimizing instance types and utilization. Over-provisioning + Long-term commitments = Wasted expenses
2.	Shared Responsibility, Not Silos	Cloud costs are everyone's business, and engineering, finance, and product must collaborate to optimize them. Automation enables this by making cost data visible and actionable across teams
3.	Showback before Chargeback	Start with transparency and show teams their respective usage before enforcing financial accountability mechanisms such as chargebacks. Build trust before the billing
4.	Automate at the Source	Enforce tagging, compliance, and governance during deployment (via IaC), not after. Shift-left to prevent waste, not clean it up
5.	Forecast with Context, Not Just History	Combine historical spend with business drivers (e.g., product launches, seasonality) for accurate predictions. Garbage in, garbage out
6.	Tagging Is the Foundation of Visibility	No tags = no cost allocation, no accountability, no automation. Consistent, automated tagging is non-negotiable

7.	Automate with a Human Touch	Tools like Netflix's Janitor Monkey notify owners before deletion. Automation should empower, not alienate
8.	Measure What Matters	Track unit costs (for example, cost per transaction, cost per user) to align cloud spend with business outcomes
9.	Start Small, Scale with Success	Automate one use case (for example, tagging in dev), measure savings, and share wins. Momentum beats mandates
10.	Treat Cloud as a Living Ecosystem	Resources spin up and down dynamically. Your cost controls must be just as dynamic–adaptive, self-healing, and continuously optimized

Table 8.1: *Foundational Principles of FinOps Practice*

The table above outlines the core operational principles that guide effective cloud financial management.

Exam Tip: *These principles map directly to the FinOps Certification Syllabus. Master them to obtain an excellent score across all the domains.*

Certification Syllabus Breakdown: How This Chapter Maps to the Exam

The FinOps certification exam evaluates your ability to apply automation and financial governance across six core domains. This chapter equips you with the knowledge and real-world context to excel in each:

Domain	**How this Prepares**
1. Organizational Alignment	Explores shared ownership models, cross-team collaboration (example, Cost Clinics), and cultural enablers like gamification and showback
2. Real-Time Decision Making	Covers cost anomaly detection, short-interval forecasting, and alerting–enabling rapid intervention before overspending occurs
3. Performance Tracking & Benchmarking	Details forecasting accuracy (e.g., 95% with Prophet), variance analysis, and KPIs like cost per unit
4. Cloud Usage Optimization	Focuses on rightsizing, lifecycle automation, tagging, and waste elimination–core automation use cases
5. Cloud Rate Optimization	Explains how forecasting enables smarter Reserved Instance and Savings Plan purchases to maximize discounts

6. Workload Management & Automation	Deep dives into tools (Terraform, Ansible, Cloud Custodian), CI/CD enforcement, and policy-as-code–automation in action

Table 8.2: *FinOps Certification Domains and Chapter Preparation*

The table above outlines the six core domains of the FinOps certification and explains how this chapter prepares you for them.

Common Pitfalls and How to Avoid Them

Here are some common mistakes candidates make during the exam–and how to steer clear of them:

Ignoring Unit Economics: From Cost Cutting to Value Optimization

Focusing solely on reducing cloud expenses without understanding the business value it brings is a classic pitfall that can backfire. A team might proudly report a 30% reduction in costs after shutting down underutilized instances, only to discover that those instances supported a critical data pipeline that had fed real-time customer recommendations. Doing so ultimately degrades user experience and reduces conversion rates. This is where unit economics becomes essential. Instead of asking "*How can we spend less?*", a FinOps team should ask "*How much does it cost to serve one customer, process a single transaction, and deliver one feature?*"

Unit economics ties cloud costs directly to business outcomes, such as cost per active user, cost per API call, or cost per checkout. For example, an e-commerce platform finds that its cloud cost per order is $0.45 during peak season. With these numbers, engineers can evaluate whether a new caching layer that reduces latency by 200ms is worth an additional $0.05 per order. This happens while the finance team gains clarity on ROI, and product teams prioritize features that improve performance without blowing the budget.

Why this works better: Unit economics transforms cloud cost from a technical line item into a strategic KPI. It enables data-driven trade-offs, aligns engineering efforts with business goals, and fosters accountability. When costs are contextualized by value, teams stop seeing FinOps as a cost-cutting exercise and start viewing it as a tool for innovation and growth. This is the hallmark of a mature FinOps practice, where cloud spend is not minimized, but is optimized instead for maximum business impact.

Overlooking Tagging Strategies: Building a Foundation for Accountability and Value Attribution

Poor or inconsistent tagging is more than just a data hygiene issue as it is a fundamental barrier to financial accountability and strategic decision-making. Without a standardized tagging strategy, cloud costs remain a black box. Finance cannot allocate spend to departments, engineering cannot identify waste, and leadership will not be able to see which projects are driving value. Worse, ad-hoc tagging can lead to misattribution, such as charging a shared DevOps tool to the marketing budget simply because someone used "marketing" in the tag name.

The solution is not just automation, but collaborative tagging governance. Successful organizations involve finance, engineering, product, and security teams in designing a minimal and meaningful tag schema, which typically includes labels such as **owner**, **project**, **environment**, **cost-center**, and **application**. This cross-functional alignment ensures that tags reflect real business structures and ownership models. For instance, tagging a resource with **`owner=product-team-alpha`** and **`project=checkout-redesign`** allows finance to track the complete cost of a strategic initiative and empowers the team to optimize within their budget.

Why this works better: When tagging is treated as a shared language rather than a technical requirement, it becomes a powerful tool for cost-to-value mapping. It enables showback reports that show business owners exactly what they're spending and why. Over time, this transparency builds trust, reduces disputes, and allows organizations to move beyond simple cost allocation to value attribution—answering not just "*Who spent it?*" but "*What did we get for it?*" This is the foundation of advanced FinOps maturity.

Rushing Commitment Purchases: The Critical Importance of Rightsizing First

One of the most common—and costly—mistakes in cloud financial management is purchasing Reserved Instances (RIs) or Savings Plans before rightsizing infrastructure. Teams, eager to lock in discounts, often commit to large, long-term contracts based on current instance types, only to later discover that those instances are significantly over-provisioned. For example, committing to three years of **m5.2xlarge** instances when **m5.large** would suffice can waste tens of thousands of dollars in avoidable spend.

The right approach is rightsizing before commitment. Use tools like AWS Compute Optimizer, Azure Advisor, or GCP Recommender to analyze historical utilization and identify opportunities to downsize or switch to more cost-effective instance families.

Only after ensuring that your workloads are optimized should you make long-term commitments. This two-step process–optimize, then commit–maximizes discount efficiency and minimizes financial risk.

Why this works better: Rightsizing first ensures that you are not paying for capacity you do not need. It turns commitment discounts from a gamble into a calculated investment. For example, a company that rightsized 500 VMs before purchasing Savings Plans reduced its compute costs by 42%–compared to the 20% they expected from commitments alone. By aligning procurement with actual usage, organizations achieve sustainable savings rather than short-term wins. This disciplined approach is a hallmark of mature FinOps teams and is directly tied to higher ROI on cloud investments.

Underestimating Collaboration: FinOps as a Shared Responsibility

Treating FinOps as a finance team's responsibility–or conversely, leaving it entirely to engineers–is a recipe for failure. When finance owns cloud costs but lacks technical context, they may impose arbitrary budget cuts that hinder innovation. When engineering owns it but ignores financial impact, they may over-provision for performance without considering cost. The most effective FinOps practices are collaborative by design, blending technical expertise with financial acumen and business strategy.

This begins with shared ownership models. Establish cross-functional FinOps teams that include members from engineering, finance, product, and security. Host regular "Cost Clinics" where engineers present their resource plans and receive feedback from finance. Use showback reports–not chargeback–to foster transparency without blame. Gamify savings with leaderboards, and celebrate wins that balance performance, cost, and value.

Why this works better: When all stakeholders are involved, cloud cost becomes a shared KPI rather than a point of conflict. Engineers learn to think like owners, finance gains trust in technical decisions, and product teams can prioritize initiatives based on true cost-to-value ratios. This culture of collaboration enables proactive cost governance, where decisions are made jointly and aligned with business goals. Ultimately, FinOps is not a role or a tool–it is a practice of collective accountability that empowers organizations to innovate responsibly and scale sustainably.

Final Insight: From Cost Allocation to Business Value

The ultimate goal of FinOps is not just to allocate costs accurately, but to associate them with business outcomes. Advanced organizations go beyond tagging and reporting to answer strategic questions such as the following ones:

- *How much cloud spend is tied to customer acquisition?*
- *What is the ROI of our new AI feature?*
- *Are we getting more value per dollar this quarter than last?*

By linking cloud costs to business value, you transform FinOps from a defensive cost-control function into a strategic enabler of innovation and growth. This is the true power of automation, data, and collaboration working together.

Practice Questions: FinOps Certification Preparation

Test your knowledge across the four key areas of the FinOps Framework. Each section includes scenario-based and conceptual questions to reinforce learning and prepare you for the certification exam.

Domain 1: Understand Usage and Cost

This section focuses on gathering, organizing, and making cloud cost and usage data visible across the organization. It includes tagging, cost allocation, anomaly detection, and real-time observability—ensuring everyone has access to accurate, timely data.

1. Who is responsible for monitoring and taking ownership of cloud utilization and expenses?
    a. Finance
    b. The FinOps team
    c. Technology teams
    d. Everyone
2. What is the primary purpose of anomaly detection in cloud cost management?
    a. To identify unused resources
    b. To detect unexpected spikes in cloud spending
    c. To forecast future cloud usage
    d. To allocate costs across teams

3. True/False: Creating a shared vocabulary (for example, standard tags, cost centers) reduces miscommunication between teams.
4. What is the foundational step in achieving cost visibility?
   a. Purchasing Reserved Instances
   b. Implementing automated scaling
   c. Enforcing consistent tagging
   d. Building dashboards in Tableau
5. Which tool capability supports real-time cost observability by enforcing tagging at deployment time?
   a. AWS Budgets
   b. Terraform with policy checks
   c. Grafana
   d. Slack bot

Domain 2: Quantify Business Value

This section connects cloud costs to business units and owners. It includes forecasting, unit economics, showback/chargeback models, and benchmarking–helping organizations understand not just *how much* they spend, but *what value* they get in return.

6. What changes when variable cloud spending becomes the norm?
   a. Engineers can buy and use only what they need at any given moment.
   b. Costs will decrease over time.
   c. Finance always controls costs before they are incurred.
   d. Budgets become fixed and rigid.
7. Which term best explains unit economics in FinOps?
   a. Incremental cost of a new service once existing costs are known
   b. Blended cost of individual compute instances across accounts
   c. Comparison of total cloud costs to produce a given unit of benefit

8. What is the main goal of organizational alignment in FinOps?
    a. To centralize decision-making authority
    b. To foster collaboration between finance, technology, and business teams
    c. To reduce cloud costs by 50%
    d. To enforce strict budget controls
9. True/False: Variance analysis compares actual cloud spending against forecasts.
10. Which metric best aligns engineering and finance teams?
    a. Cost per deployment
    b. Lines of code
    c. Employee retention
    d. Uptime percentage

Domain 3: Optimize Usage and Cost

This section covers technical and financial optimization, which includes rightsizing, lifecycle management, automation, and commitment strategies that ensure resources are used efficiently and purchased at the best possible rate.

11. Finding and removing underutilized resources is one place to start rightsizing. True or False?
12. What is the first step in rightsizing?
    a. Remove underutilized resources
    b. Forecast future usage
    c. Purchase reserved instances
    d. Negotiate discounts
13. What is the primary purpose of automated scaling?
    a. Restrict access to cloud resources
    b. Align resources with demand
    c. Standardize instance types
    d. Limit regions

14. Purchasing an Azure RI, a GCP Committed Use Discount, or committing to an AWS Savings Plan are examples of:
    a. Cloud Usage Optimization
    b. Cloud Rate Optimization
    c. Establishing a FinOps Decision and Accountability Structure
    d. Workload Management and Automation
15. What is amortization in the context of Reserved Instances?
    a. Immediate expensing of upfront costs
    b. Spreading costs over time
    c. A chargeback method
    d. Budget forecasting

Domain 4: Manage the FinOps Practice

This section focuses on the people, processes, and culture needed to sustain FinOps. It includes governance, collaboration, continuous improvement, and embedding FinOps into organizational workflows.

16. What is the primary role of a centralized FinOps team?
    a. Approve all cloud resource requests
    b. Perform commitment purchasing activities
    c. Build CI/CD pipelines
    d. Ensure consistent patching of infrastructure
17. Which persona is primarily responsible for driving accountability and transparency in cloud spending?
    a. IT Finance Manager
    b. Product Owner
    c. Cloud Architect
    d. FinOps Champion
18. When should resources run in the cloud?
    a. Only when needed to run software
    b. Only from 8 AM to 5 PM on weekdays

   c. Slightly in advance of significant demand
   d. In multiple geographic locations for redundancy
19. True/False: Rightsizing eliminates all underutilized resources immediately.
20. Which of the following is true about anomaly definitions?
   a. Anomaly definitions are static and should not be changed.
   b. Anomalies do not need to be defined.
   c. Anomaly definitions should be continuously reviewed and refined.

Answers

1. d
2. b
3. True
4. c
5. b
6. a
7. c
8. b
9. True
10. a
11. True
12. a
13. a
14. b
15. b
16. b
17. a
18. a
19. False
20. c

Mock Exam: FinOps Certification Practice

Total Questions: 53

Prepare for success with scenario-based questions aligned to the official FinOps Framework. This mock exam reinforces key concepts in cost visibility, value quantification, optimization, and practice management, which are essential for both obtaining the certification and applying these principles to real-world scenarios.

Final Tip: *Review all the explanations to understand the reasons behind the correct answers. This exercise will encourage you to think critically while attempting questions based on scenarios and real-world decision-making.*

Domain 1: Understand Usage and Cost

This section covers the foundational practices of gathering, organizing, and making cloud cost and usage data visible. It includes tagging, cost allocation, anomaly detection, and real-time observability, which ensure that all stakeholders have access to accurate, timely data.

1. Who is responsible for monitoring and taking ownership of cloud utilization and expenses?
    a. Finance
    b. The FinOps team
    c. Technology teams
    d. Everyone
2. What is the primary goal of the “Inform” phase in FinOps?
    a. Align cloud usage with business goals
    b. Identify cost savings opportunities
    c. Ensure that teams have visibility into cloud spending
    d. Optimize cloud performance
3. True/False: A shared vocabulary reduces miscommunication between teams.
4. What is the primary purpose of a cost allocation model in FinOps?
    a. Distribute costs to cloud providers
    b. Divide costs among teams and business units

   c. Track cloud performance
   d. Calculate Return on Investment (ROI)

5. Which capability is part of Workload Management and Automation?
   a. Rightsizing
   b. Resource scheduling
   c. Variance analysis
   d. Benchmarking

6. What is the primary purpose of a FinOps dashboard?
   a. Track employee attendance
   b. Visualize real-time costs/metrics
   c. Manage CI/CD pipelines
   d. Generate contracts

7. Which domain includes anomaly detection?
   a. Real-Time Decision Making
   b. Cloud Rate Optimization
   c. Organizational Alignment
   d. Workload Management

8. What triggers a threshold alert?
   a. New cloud region activation
   b. Spending exceeds a predefined limit
   c. Resource patching
   d. Budget approval

9. True/False: Showback reports enforce chargebacks.

10. Which phase involves creating showback reports?
    a. Inform
    b. Optimize
    c. Operate
    d. All phases

11. What is the role of the Cloud Financial Analyst in a FinOps organization?
    a. Manage cloud contracts
    b. Analyze cloud cost data and identify opportunities for savings
    c. Lead cloud migration projects
    d. Develop cloud infrastructure architectures
12. Which of the following is an important consideration when choosing cloud cost management tools?
    a. They should be compatible with all cloud providers.
    b. They should automate as many tasks as possible.
    c. They should be free to use.
    d. They should provide historical data on cloud infrastructure costs.

Domain 2: Quantify Business Value

This section connects cloud costs to business outcomes. It includes forecasting, unit economics, benchmarking, and variance analysis, which help organizations understand the amount they spend and the value they get in return.

13. What is "unit economics"?
    a. Cost per customer
    b. Total cloud spend
    c. Reserved instance discounts
    d. Budget variance
14. Forecasting during the "Run" phase involves:
    a. Manual estimates
    b. Granular daily updates
    c. Annual projections
    d. Fixed budgets
15. Which domain evaluates if cloud spending aligns with strategic objectives?
    a. Organizational Alignment
    b. Performance Tracking and Benchmarking

   c. Workload Management
   d. Cloud Rate Optimization
16. True/False: Variable spending allows engineers to use only what they need.
17. Which metric aligns engineering and finance teams?
   a. Cost per deployment
   b. Lines of code
   c. Employee retention
   d. Uptime percentage
18. What is the purpose of variance analysis in FinOps?
   a. To identify opportunities for cost allocation optimization
   b. To analyze differences between forecasted and actual cloud costs
   c. To forecast cloud costs more accurately
   d. To adjust cloud resources based on performance
19. What is the purpose of benchmarking cloud spending in FinOps?
   a. To compare cloud performance across providers
   b. To track cloud spending against industry standards
   c. To optimize cloud infrastructure performance
   d. To identify the best pricing model for cloud services.
20. Which of the following is NOT part of the "Optimize" phase in FinOps?
   a. Rightsizing
   b. Cost allocation
   c. Cloud cost forecasting
   d. Reserved instance management
21. True/False: FinOps eliminates the need for budgets.
22. How frequently should the FinOps lifecycle be executed?
   a. Quarterly
   b. Yearly

   c. Continuously

   d. Once

23. True/False: A FinOps culture is only relevant to large organizations with complex cloud environments.

24. What is the final step in a FinOps lifecycle?

   a. Forecasting

   b. Optimizing

   c. Reporting

   d. Informing

Domain 3: Optimize Usage and Cost

This section focuses on technical and financial optimization features like rightsizing, lifecycle management, automation, and commitment strategies. It ensures that resources are used efficiently and purchased at the best possible rate.

25. What is the first step in rightsizing?

   a. Remove underutilized resources

   b. Forecast future usage

   c. Purchase reserved instances

   d. Negotiate discounts

26. True/False: Rightsizing eliminates all underutilized resources immediately.

27. Automated scaling reduces costs by:

   a. Restricting access

   b. Aligning resources with demand

   c. Standardizing instance types

   d. Limiting regions

28. What is a "blended rate"?

   a. Average cost across pricing models

   b. Multi-cloud spend

   c. Discounted reserved instance rates
   d. Chargeback method

29. Which team identifies consistent usage for commitment discounts?
   a. Engineering
   b. Centralized FinOps
   c. Cloud Provider
   d. Finance

30. Commitment purchases (for example, Reserved Instances) occur in which phase?
   a. Inform
   b. Optimize
   c. Operate
   d. All phases

31. Which of the following is a key objective in the "Optimize" phase?
   a. Setting up cost allocation tags
   b. Reviewing and negotiating pricing contracts
   c. Ensuring that teams are aware of their cloud usage
   d. Ensuring that cloud costs are within budget limits

32. What is the main focus of cloud financial optimization?
   a. Reducing cloud spend to a fixed amount
   b. Improving cost transparency across all teams
   c. Eliminating cloud waste without compromising performance
   d. Migrating workloads to lower-cost cloud providers

33. How do commitment purchases (for example, Reserved Instances) contribute to FinOps?
   a. They help guarantee cloud service availability.
   b. They enable companies to forecast costs more effectively.
   c. They provide discounts based on longer-term usage commitments.
   d. They allow businesses to avoid paying for underutilized resources.

34. True/False: The Operate phase prioritizes cloud over business goals.
35. What is amortization?
    a. Immediate expensing of upfront costs
    b. Spreading costs over time
    c. A chargeback method
    d. Budget forecasting
36. What is the main objective of the "Operate" phase in FinOps?
    a. Forecast future usage
    b. Maintain optimized workflows
    c. Create visibility dashboards
    d. Set budgets

Domain 4: Manage the FinOps Practice

This section covers the people, processes, and culture needed to sustain FinOps. It includes governance, collaboration, automation, and embedding FinOps into organizational workflows.

37. What is a "FinOps Champion"?
    a. Cloud provider representative
    b. Team advocate for FinOps practices
    c. Budgeting software
    d. Executive leader
38. True/False: FinOps requires disbanding the existing teams.
39. Which persona focuses on driving process improvement and efficiency in cloud financial management?
    a. FinOps Champion
    b. Cloud Architect
    c. Finance Executive
    d. Cloud Operations Manager

40. How do engineering teams contribute to FinOps practices?
    a. By handling negotiations with cloud providers
    b. By developing infrastructure automation scripts
    c. By ensuring cloud resources are provisioned according to cost optimization guidelines
    d. By managing financial forecasting and budgeting
41. True/False: A successful FinOps program requires a shift from reactive to proactive cost management.
42. What role does automation play in FinOps?
    a. It automates the creation of cloud resources.
    b. It helps identify and correct financial anomalies in real-time.
    c. It handles the forecasting of cloud resource demands.
    d. It automates the payment process to cloud providers.
43. What is the primary goal of the IT Finance Manager persona?
    a. Budget accuracy
    b. Speed of deployment
    c. Resource patching
    d. Negotiate contracts
44. True/False: A centralized FinOps team handles all the aspects of cloud financial management.
45. Which persona delivers faster product features with accurate pricing?
    a. Product Owner
    b. Finance Manager
    c. Engineer
    d. Executive Sponsor
46. What is the first step in creating a FinOps strategy?
    a. Defining a shared vocabulary across teams
    b. Developing a cost allocation model

   c. Implementing a cloud usage dashboard
   d. Setting up monthly budget reports

47. How does a FinOps culture enhance collaboration between teams?
    a. By centralizing all cloud-related decisions
    b. By providing clear visibility into cloud costs and usage
    c. By making teams more responsible for budget approvals
    d. By focusing only on cloud-related technology decisions
48. The FinOps Iron Triangle trade-offs are:
    a. Quality, Speed, Cost
    b. Inform, Optimize, Operate
    c. Budget, Forecast, Report
    d. People, Process, Tools
49. What is the primary benefit of using cloud financial automation tools?
    a. Automate the deployment of cloud resources
    b. Provide real-time cost insights and alerts
    c. Automatically negotiate contracts with cloud providers
    d. Speed up cloud migration processes
50. Which tool is commonly used to enforce tagging policies programmatically?
    a. Jenkins
    b. Terraform
    c. Grafana
    d. Tableau
51. Which forecasting tool is best suited for datasets with strong seasonality?
    a. LSTM
    b. Prophet
    c. Linear Regression
    d. Decision Tree

52. Why is tagging critical in cloud cost management?
    a. It reduces cloud provider costs.
    b. It enables accurate cost allocation and accountability.
    c. It speeds up deployments.
    d. It improves application performance.
53. True/False: Tagging strategies require input from all teams.

Final Tip: *Treat your cloud like a living ecosystem, not a static spreadsheet. Nurture it with the right tools, and it will fuel innovation for years to come.*

Answers

1. d
2. c
3. True
4. b
5. b
6. b
7. a
8. b
9. False
10. a
11. b
12. b
13. a
14. b
15. b
16. True
17. a
18. b

19. b
20. b
21. False
22. c
23. False
24. c
25. c
26. False
27. b
28. a
29. b
30. b
31. b
32. c
33. c
34. False
35. b
36. b
37. b
38. False
39. a
40. c
41. True
42. b
43. a
44. False
45. a
46. a

47. b
48. a
49. b
50. b
51. b
52. b
53. True

Conclusion

This chapter provided a comprehensive overview of the certification exam, including a detailed breakdown of its sections, practical tips to avoid common pitfalls, and realistic practice tests with in-depth explanations. By engaging with these materials, you will not only gain clarity on the exam structure but also develop the confidence and strategy needed to perform effectively on the test day. The next chapter is on Real-World Case Study and Best Practices.

Key Terms

- **Shared Responsibility Model**
- Cloud cost management is everyone's responsibility, not just finance or engineering teams
- **Key Takeaway:** *Finance tracks, engineering tocks, business talks*
- **FinOps Lifecycle Phases**
  - The lifecycle includes three phases: Inform, Optimize , and Operate
  - **Key Takeaway:** *Inform first, Optimize second, Operate always*
- **Rightsizing Before Commitments**
  - Always rightsize resources before making commitment purchases like Reserved Instances
  - **Key Takeaway:** *Rightsizing first, Commitments second*
- **Continuous Iteration**
  - The FinOps lifecycle is iterative and should be run continuously, not just once or quarterly
  - **Key Takeaway:** *Run it often, keep it fresh*

- **Unit Economics**
  - Link cloud costs to business value using unit economics (for example, cost per transaction or customer)
  - **Key Takeaway:** *Cost per unit = Value delivered*
- **Iron Triangle Trade-Offs**
  - Balance Quality, Speed, and Cost when making cloud decisions
  - **Key Takeaway:** *Quality, Speed, Cost–pick two!*
- **Showback vs. Chargeback**
  - Showback provides visibility without penalties, while chargebacks enforce accountability
  - **Key Takeaway:** *Showback = Transparency, Chargeback = Accountability*
- **Benchmarking and Variance Analysis**
  - Benchmark performance against KPIs and conduct variance analysis to identify discrepancies
  - **Key Takeaway:** *Compare to compete, benchmark to budget*
- **Tagging Strategies**
  - Tags ensure accurate cost allocation across teams and require collaboration
  - **Key Takeaway:** *Tag it right, track it tight*
- **Automation Saves Time**
  - Automate scaling, scheduling, and anomaly detection to optimize efficiency
  - **Key Takeaway:** *Automate to elevate*
- **Amortization**
  - Spread upfront costs (like Reserved Instances) over time to reflect their benefits
  - **Key Takeaway:** *Spread the cost, share the benefit*
- **Anomalies Evolve**
  - Anomaly definitions should be reviewed and refined regularly as usage patterns change
  - **Key Takeaway:** *Alert early, act fast*
- **Cloud Rate Optimization**
  - Use discounts (for example, Reserved Instances, Spot Instances) to reduce per-unit costs
  - **Key Takeaway:** *Spot the savings, preempt the waste*

- **Workload Management**
  - Run resources only when needed and schedule them efficiently
  - **Key Takeaway:** *Use what you need, when you need it*
- **Reporting Completes the Cycle**
  - Reporting summarizes financial performance and informs future decisions
  - **Key Takeaway:** *Report to improve and repeat to refine*

Final Review Strategy: How to Approach the Exam

Preparing for the FinOps certification exam is not just about memorizing facts–it is about thinking like a FinOps practitioner. The exam tests your ability to apply principles across people, processes, and technology in real-world scenarios. Use this strategy to stay focused, make better decisions, and maximize your score.

1. **Skim through All Questions First**
   - Do not dive in immediately. Take 5–10 minutes to skim through all the questions.
   - Flag the questions that seem ambiguous or complex.
   - Answer the straightforward questions first to build momentum and save time to tackle the tougher ones later.
2. **Use the Process of Elimination**
   - For multiple-choice questions, eliminate the obviously incorrect options first.
   - Watch for extreme signifiers like *always*, *never*, *only*, or *all*. These are the red flags in FinOps, where context and balance matter.
   - Ask yourself: *Does this promote shared ownership? Is it scalable? Does it align with FinOps principles?*
3. **Anchor in the FinOps Iron Triangle: Cost, Quality, Time**

In the practice of FinOps, strategic decision-making often involves navigating competing priorities. The FinOps Iron Triangle provides a critical framework for this, framing every significant cloud-related decision as a balance between three fundamental dimensions: Cost, Quality, and Time. When a question seems ambiguous or a trade-off appears necessary, systematically evaluating which corner of the triangle it prioritizes will bring immediate clarity and guide you toward a balanced, business-aligned outcome.

Whenever a question feels unclear, ask yourself which dimension it is prioritizing. You can refer to the following table to refine your approach:

Dimension	Questions You Must Ask
Cost	Is this about reducing waste, optimizing spend, or forecasting?
Quality	Does this impact performance, reliability, user experience, or compliance?
Time	Is speed of delivery, response time, or deployment velocity the focus?

***Table 8.3**: The FinOps Iron Triangle Framework*

This table defines the three core dimensions of the FinOps Iron Triangle and provides guiding questions for each.

· FinOps decisions are about balancing trade-offs, not maximizing one dimension at the expense of others.

For example:

- A question about Reserved Instances? That's Cost (savings), but consider Time (commitment length) and Quality (can you resize later if needs change?)
- A question about auto-scaling during a product launch? That's Time (responding to demand) and Quality (maintaining performance), but must be balanced with Cost (avoiding overspending)

This triangle is your decision compass–use it to eliminate extreme or unbalanced answers.

4. **Map to the FinOps Lifecycle**: **`Inform` → `Optimize` → `Operate`**

If you are unsure when or who owns a task, think about the FinOps lifecycle:

- **Inform:** Visibility, tagging, showback, forecasting, anomaly detection
- **Optimize:** Rightsizing, automation, commitment purchases, rate optimization
- **Operate:** Continuous monitoring, lifecycle management, governance, collaboration

This helps you to choose the most mature, collaborative, and realistic answer–especially for scenario-based questions.

5. **Think in Terms of Domains, Not Isolated Tasks**

The FinOps Framework has four domains–not steps, but parallel outcomes:

a. Understand Usage and Cost: Gathering data, tagging, cost allocation

b. Quantify Business Value: Forecasting, unit economics, benchmarking

c. Optimize Usage and Cost: Rightsizing, automation, anomaly management

d. Manage the FinOps Practice: Education, collaboration, tooling, continuous improvement

Before answering, ask: *Which domain does this question belong to*? This helps you avoid choosing technically correct but contextually wrong answers.

6. **Relate Ambiguous Questions to Personas**

If a question asks *who* should do something, think of the FinOps personas:

- IT Finance Manager → Budgeting, forecasting, reporting
- Product Owner → Balancing speed, cost, and value
- Engineer → Building efficient, cost-aware systems
- FinOps Champion → Advocating for best practices across teams

Choose the answer that reflects shared responsibility, not siloed ownership.

Final Tip: Treat Your Cloud Like a Living Ecosystem

Do not manage your cloud like a static spreadsheet with fixed line items. Treat it as a dynamic, evolving ecosystem that constantly adapts to demand, innovation, and business goals.

With the right blend of automation, collaboration, and continuous improvement, your cloud can become a self-optimizing engine for innovation and not a cost management center.

It is important to remember that FinOps is not about cutting costs, but maximizing value.

By mastering the Iron Triangle, living the lifecycle, and applying these strategies, you will be ready to implement FinOps principles in the real world and succeed in the exam.

CHAPTER 9
Real-World Case Study and Best Practices

Introduction

In today's cloud-first world, managing financial operations effectively is not just about spreadsheets and dashboards; it is about people. It is also about teams coming together across departments to make smarter decisions, align costs with value, and build sustainable practices that scale.

FinOps has emerged as a powerful framework for doing exactly that. But while understanding its principles is one thing, seeing how it plays out in real companies—with real people, real budgets, and real business pressures—is where the true learning happens.

In this chapter, we take you inside the journeys of real organizations—from retail giants to fast-growing startups—as they implemented FinOps to regain control over their cloud spend, improve visibility, and drive accountability. These are not just case studies, but stories of transformation, collaboration, and leadership.

Structure

We will also explore how to apply what these companies learned to your own organization, whether you are a part of a small team or a global enterprise. Along the way, we will cover:

- Strategies for scaling FinOps across large organizations
- Emerging practices for managing AI costs
- The rise of FOCUS™ for SaaS transparency
- And how earning your FinOps certification can unlock new career paths

Let us begin with the first case study about a major retail chain that was drowning in cloud costs after a rushed migration.

Real-Life Case Study: Human-Centered FinOps Journeys

The Challenge: Rapid Growth with Cloud Cost Outpacing Visibility

Logz.io[1], an observability platform based in Israel, was experiencing fast growth with increasingly complex infrastructure. Their engineering and operations teams were deploying resources across multiple services, but they lacked:

- Clear **cost attribution** by product, feature, or team
- Consistent reporting tools to show how design decisions impacted cloud costs
- A mechanism to forecast cloud spending reliably across different business units

The finance and engineering teams needed to see exactly where and how spending was happening, so they could make informed decisions. Without that, cost overruns and surprises were becoming increasingly frequent.

The Solution: Visibility, Attribution, and Dashboards

To address these challenges, Logz.io partnered with **Finout** to establish a robust FinOps practice. The key steps included:

1. **Virtual Tags and Granular Attribution**
    - Finout helped Logz.io adopt *virtual tagging*, enabling them to tag up to **98% of AWS spending** to specific workloads, features, or product lines.
    - This allowed teams to see the cost impact of their work in near real time.
2. **Shared Dashboards**
    - Dashboards were built for each business unit, showing spend by service and by feature.
    - Engineers could see how their design or code changes would affect cost metrics.

[1] *Source: Logz.io & Finout Case Study – AWS Partner Success Story*

3. **Faster Reporting and Alerts**
    - What used to take days or weeks to report could now be generated in minutes.
    - Alerts and thresholds were set up so teams would be notified when spending deviated from expectations.

The Outcomes: Cost Savings + Better Accountability

Logz.io's implementation delivered measurable improvements:

- **30% reduction** in AWS spending overall
- **98% of cloud costs** now accurately attributed to specific workloads or teams
- **Significant time savings** – reports that took days now take minutes
- **Improved alignment** between engineering and finance, with increased transparency in decision-making

Implementing FinOps: A Cross-Functional Practice

Liberty Mutual built a centralized FinOps practice focused on collaboration, automation, and continuous improvement. These initiatives include the following features:

1. **Unified Cost Visibility**
    - Built a centralized data lake using AWS Cost and Usage Reports (CUR) and Amazon Redshift
    - Aggregated data across 1,000+ AWS accounts for granular analysis
2. **Automated Tagging and Policy Enforcement**
    - Used AWS Service Catalog and Control Tower to enforce tagging at provisioning time
    - Integrated Open Policy Agent (OPA) into CI/CD pipelines to block non-compliant deployments
    - Required tags: `owner`, `project`, `environment`, `cost-center`
3. **Showback Reporting and Accountability**
    - Launched monthly showback reports delivered via Amazon QuickSight dashboards

    - Reports showed spend by team, project, and service—enabling engineers to optimize their own usage
    - Introduced unit economics (for example, cost per policy quote) to link spend to business outcomes
4. **Forecasting and Anomaly Detection**
    - Developed predictive models using historical spend and business drivers (for example, marketing campaigns)
    - Used CloudWatch + Lambda + Slack alerts to detect cost anomalies in real time
    - One alert caught a misconfigured auto-scaling group within hours, preventing a $150K overspend
5. **FinOps Culture and Education**
    - Established a FinOps Center of Excellence (CoE) to train engineers and finance teams
    - Hosted "Cost Clinics" where teams reviewed spending patterns and received optimization advice
    - Created a gamified leaderboard to recognize top cost-saving teams

Key Outcomes

Following the implementation of a structured FinOps operating model, the organization achieved measurable improvements in financial accountability, cost efficiency, and cross-team collaboration. The following table summarizes the most significant results:

Outcome	Impact
90%+ tagging compliance	Achieved within 12 months through automation and enforcement
$10M+ annual savings	From rightsizing, reserved instance optimization, and waste elimination
Improved forecasting accuracy	Within 10% of actuals across business units
Stronger engineering-finance collaboration	Engineers now proactively optimize costs

***Table 9.1**: Key Outcomes of the FinOps Implementation*

This table summarizes the most significant financial and operational results achieved after establishing a structured FinOps operating model.

Scaling FinOps in Large Organizations

Scaling FinOps beyond pilot programs can be complex, especially in enterprises with thousands of users and multiple cloud environments. According to the **FinOps Framework**, success requires iteration across the **Inform, Optimize, and Operate** phases, while staying true to the **FinOps Principles** of shared accountability, collaboration, and maintaining centralized governance with distributed execution.

Here are five strategies that are aligned with FinOps best practices:

- **Start Small, Think Big (Operate):** Pilot FinOps in one department or product team before scaling enterprise-wide. This iterative approach mirrors the **crawl-walk-run maturity model** endorsed by FinOps which ensure that the lessons learned will guide the broader rollout.
- **Build a Center of Excellence (CoE) (Operate):** A CoE provides governance and consistency, acting as the nucleus for **standards, best practices, and enablement**. This reflects the FinOps principle of **a centralized team driving practices while enabling distributed accountability**.
- **Leverage Role-Based Access and Reporting (Inform):** FinOps highlights the importance of tailoring reporting for different personas: executives, finance, product, and engineering. Right-sizing dashboards ensures stakeholders engage with the data relevant to their decisions.
- **Implement Governance Frameworks (Operate/Optimize):** Standards around **tagging, budgets, and resource lifecycle management** are critical FinOps practices. Governance ensures consistency while enabling **accountability across teams**, which reflects the FinOps principle of "everyone takes ownership of their cloud usage."
- **Measure and Iterate (Inform → Optimize → Operate):** FinOps is inherently cyclical. Setting baselines, tracking KPIs, and iterating aligns with the FinOps principle of **timely, accessible reporting** and the need to **continuously improve practices as maturity grows**.

Emerging Practice: FinOps for Generative AI and Machine Learning

As generative AI and tools such as LLM-powered chatbots and custom-trained models become central to business operations, managing costs effectively has become a top priority. Unlike traditional cloud workloads, AI introduces unique complexities due to:

- Unpredictable usage patterns like sudden inference spikes

- Specialized hardware like GPU/TPU instances that are 5–10x more expensive
- Experimental development cycles with high failure rates
- Lack of standardized cost attribution across teams and models

Without proper governance, AI projects can quickly become cost black holes that consume budgets without a clear ROI.

Applying FinOps Principles to AI

Organizations are adapting the FinOps Framework to bring visibility, accountability, and optimization to AI workloads. As generative AI and machine learning workloads consume an increasing share of cloud budgets, applying FinOps disciplines becomes critical to managing their unique cost dynamics. The following table outlines how core FinOps domains are being adapted specifically for AI.

FinOps Domain	**AI Application**
Understand Usage and Cost	Track spend by model, project, team, and phase (training vs. inference)
Quantify Business Value	Measure cost per inference, accuracy per dollar, or ROI of AI features
Optimize Usage & Cost	Right-size GPU instances, use spot instances for training, cache responses
Manage the FinOps Practice	Establish AI cost policies, educate data science teams, integrate with MLOps

***Table 9.2**: Applying FinOps Principles to AI Workload Management*

This table demonstrates how organizations are adapting core FinOps domains to manage and optimize cloud spending for artificial intelligence and machine learning workloads.

Visibility into AI Spend

Use tools such as AWS Cost Allocation Tags, GCP's AI Expenditure Reports, or third-party platforms like Weights and Biases and OctoAI to track costs across the following areas:

- Model training jobs
- Inference endpoints
- Embedding pipelines
- LLM API calls like OpenAI and Anthropic

Tag all AI resources with **`model-name`**, **`model-version`**, **`use-case`**, and **`owner`** to enable granular reporting.

Accountability through Ownership

Assign ownership of AI projects to product teams or business units, instead of just data scientists. Implement tagging strategies that capture:

- **`team=marketing-ai`**
- **`phase=training`**
- **`model-version=v2`**
- **`environment=production`**

This enables showback reports that answer: "*How much did our customer support chatbot cost last month?*"

Continuous Optimization

AI is not "set and forget." FinOps teams should:

- **Compare cost-performance tradeoffs:** Is a smaller, cheaper model "good enough"?
- Use caching for repetitive LLM queries like FAQ responses
- Compress models or use quantization to reduce inference costs
- **Hybrid strategies:** Train on-prem, infer in the cloud

For example, according to Redmore Studio, enterprises with high query volumes (e.g., over 1 billion queries/month) have reported that RAG deployments can **cut operational costs by 40-60%** by reducing inference loads and eliminating waste in model usage. Redmore Studio

Forecasting and Budgeting for AI

Traditional forecasting fails with AI due to experimentation. Instead, use scenario-based models like the ones mentioned here:

- **Low:** Baseline inference for 10K users
- **Mid:** Expected growth + new features
- **High:** Viral adoption such as when a chatbot goes viral

Set the following guardrails:

- $500/month cap on sandbox projects
- Approval required for >$5K/month in production

Emerging Trends in FinOps for AI

- **Model-level cost attribution:** Track spend per model, not just per team
- **AI-as-a-Service (AIaaS) cost analysis:** Compare managed vs. self-hosted models
- **Carbon footprint monitoring:** Align AI usage with Cloud Sustainability goals
- **Natural language querying:** Let the finance department ask questions like, "*Show me all LLM costs from* Q2" via AI-powered dashboards

Remember that the same FinOps principles apply here as well, albeit with a different context. Use the Iron Triangle to evaluate the following trade-offs:

- *Cost* of GPU instances
- *Quality* of model output
- *Time* to deploy and scale

Final Thought: AI Needs FinOps, Not Chaos

Generative AI is not just a technical innovation, it is a financial risk and opportunity. Without FinOps, AI projects spiral into uncontrolled spending. With it, organizations can innovate responsibly, measure value, and scale sustainably.

You must treat AI like any other cloud workload: tag it, track it, optimize it, and own it.

Emerging Standard: FOCUS™ Adoption

As SaaS continues to grow, so does the complexity of tracking and optimizing these expenses. According to recent FinOps surveys, SaaS now accounts for 20–30% of total cloud-related spend, and is rising continuously. Yet, unlike IaaS/PaaS platforms, most SaaS vendors provide inconsistent, fragmented, or opaque usage and cost reports, making it nearly impossible for FinOps teams to gain full visibility.

To address this challenge, the FinOps Foundation introduced FOCUS™ (FinOps Open Cost and Usage Specification)–an open-source, vendor-agnostic standard that enables SaaS providers to deliver consistent, normalized cost, and usage data in a structured format.

Think of FOCUS™ as the "CSV of cloud billing" for SaaS, a common language that allows buyers to consolidate, analyze, and act on subscription data across dozens of vendors.

Exam Tip: FOCUS™ Is a High-Value Emerging Topic

Expect at least one question on FOCUS™ in the FinOps certification exam.

The key concepts to know:

- FOCUS™ is a data specification, not a tool or platform.
- It enables standardized fields such as **`BilledCost`**, **`UsageQuantity`**, **`AmortizedCost`**, and **`ServiceName`**.
- It supports cross-vendor consolidation, forecasting, and chargeback/showback.
- It aligns with the Data Ingestion and Examine as well as Showback capabilities in the FinOps Framework.

Note: FOCUS™ *reduces manual work and increases trust in data—a core goal of the Understand Usage and Cost domain.*

Why FOCUS™ Matters

Before FOCUS™, FinOps teams spent countless hours manually normalizing CSV exports from different SaaS vendors—each with unique formats, currencies, and units of measure. This led to delays, errors, and poor decision-making.

With FOCUS™, organizations gain:

Benefit	**Impact**
Unified Billing and Usage Data	Standardized schema enables automated ingestion into data lakes and dashboards
Transparency and Predictability	Clear cost breakdowns improve budgeting, forecasting, and vendor negotiations
Actionable Insights	Plug FOCUS™ datasets directly into tools like Tableau, Power BI, or Snowflake
Real-Time Monitoring	Ingest data daily (or hourly) to detect usage spikes or over-provisioning
Cross-Provider Comparability	Compare SaaS offerings not just by features, but by cost per user, cost per transaction, or ROI

***Table* 9.3**: *Benefits of the FOCUS™ Model for FinOps Operations*

This table outlines the key benefits and organizational impacts of implementing the standardized FOCUS™ framework for cloud and SaaS financial management.

"The lack of standardization in SaaS billing has been a long-standing challenge for finance and operations teams. By adopting the FOCUS™ framework and automating reconciliation processes, organizations have gained better visibility and efficiency in managing cloud and SaaS expenditures. Similar to how **Papaya Global** achieved a **90% reduction in manual bank reconciliation tasks** using automation, adopting FOCUS™ helps reduce manual reconciliation efforts and enhances cost transparency across business portfolios." – *Source: Papaya Global Case Study, ledge.* co.

How to Encourage FOCUS™ Adoption with Vendors

FOCUS™ only works if vendors adopt it. As a FinOps practitioner, you can drive change by advocating for standardization in your vendor relationships by adopting the following practices:

1. **Start with a Letter Requesting Conformance**

   Use the official FOCUS™ request template from the FinOps Foundation to formally ask your SaaS providers to support the specification. Link: https://www.finops.org/focus

2. **Highlight Benefits for the Vendor**

   Explain the vendors about how FOCUS™ can help them too in the following ways:

   - **Grants Improved Customer Satisfaction:** Easier integration with customer FinOps systems
   - **Provides Competitive Differentiation:** Positioned as a modern, transparent vendor
   - **Reduces Support Burden:** Fewer questions about billing discrepancies

3. **Leverage Industry Momentum:** Point to early adopters such as AWS, Google Cloud, and Datadog, which already support FOCUS™ for their SaaS offerings. Show vendors that this is not a niche request, but an industry shift

4. **Work with Procurement:** Collaborate with your procurement or sourcing team to include FOCUS™ compliance in RFPs, contracts, and renewal negotiations. Make it a "nice-to-have" today so it becomes a "must-have" tomorrow

Alignment with FinOps Capabilities

FOCUS™ directly supports multiple capabilities in the FinOps Framework, including:

- **Data Ingestion**: Enables structured, queryable datasets across providers
- **Examine and Showback**: Powers accurate cost allocation and reporting
- **Forecasting**: Provides reliable input for SaaS spend models
- **Rate Optimization**: Facilitates vendor comparisons and renewal strategies

It also strengthens FinOps Practice Operations by reducing manual work and improving data quality.

Final Thought: From Chaos to Clarity

SaaS spending does not have to be a black box. With FOCUS™, organizations can bring the same level of financial control to SaaS that they have achieved with IaaS through standardization, automation, and transparency.

Beyond Certification

Congratulations on earning your FinOps certification! But this is not the end; it is the beginning of a deeper journey, where you move from understanding principles to driving transformation.

FinOps is not a static credential. It is a practice, a mindset, and a career accelerator. As cloud continues to evolve, so too will your role in shaping how organizations use it responsibly, sustainably, and strategically.

Here is how to turn your certification into a lasting impact:

1. **Advance Your Career with Specialized Roles**

   Certified FinOps professionals are in high demand across industries. Your skills span across departments like finance, engineering, and business, making you a critical player in cloud decision-making.

   Emerging roles include:

   - **FinOps Analyst:** Dive into cost data, build forecasts, and identify optimization opportunities
   - **Cloud Financial Manager:** Own the cloud budget, lead showback/chargeback programs, and align spend with business outcomes
   - **Cloud Cost Optimization Engineer:** Design and automate rightsizing, commitment strategies, and anomaly detection at scale

- **FinOps Consultant:** Help organizations mature their practice, from initial visibility to full automation

These roles offer competitive salaries, cross-functional influence, and a clear path to leadership in cloud strategy, digital transformation, or platform engineering.

2. **Explore Consulting and Freelancing**

With remote work and cloud adoption on the rise, startups and mid-market companies often lack in-house FinOps expertise but they need it to scale efficiently.

Your certification positions you as a trusted advisor since you will be able to:

- Offer fractional FinOps services to multiple clients
- Build automated cost governance packages such as tagging policies and anomaly alerts
- Partner with MSPs (Managed Service Providers) or cloud consultancies

Platforms such as Toptal, Upwork, or even LinkedIn can help you connect with organizations looking for on-demand expertise to avoid overspending and build accountability.

Tip: *Start by offering free workshops or audits to build case studies and credibility.*

3. **Become a Thought Leader:** As you apply FinOps in real-world scenarios, your experience becomes valuable to the broader community.

Share your knowledge through:

- Blogs and articles on platforms such as Medium, Dev.to, or your company's site
- Podcasts and webinars that invite both practitioners and domain experts
- Conference talks on forums such as FinOps Pro, AWS re:Invent, KubeCon, and local meetups

Speaking does not require perfection, it requires perspective. Whether it is about how you reduced waste by 40% or how you got engineers to care about cost, your story can inspire others.

4. **Lead Internally: Advocate, Mentor, and Build Communities**

Some of the most impactful FinOps work happens within your own organization.

You can:

- Launch a FinOps guild–a cross-functional group focused on shared learning and best practices
- Host "Cost Clinics" where teams review their spending with FinOps guidance
- Mentor junior engineers on cost-aware development
- Partner with finance to co-develop showback reports that drive better decisions

These efforts build trust, break down silos, and embed FinOps into your company's culture–not just its tools.

Pro Tip: *Recognize wins publicly.* A *simple* "*Team* X *saved* $50K *this quarter*" *email from leadership can fuel momentum.*

5. **Innovate: Shape the Future of Cloud Economics**

   Your fluency in technology and finance will make you uniquely qualified to build the next generation of cloud tools.

   Consider moving into the following arenas:

   - Product management for cost optimization, observability, or sustainability platforms
   - Engineering roles focused on cloud efficiency like auto-scaling and serverless cost modeling
   - Research and development in AI-driven forecasting or carbon-aware computing

   Many leading FinOps tools were built by practitioners who saw a gap and said, "*There has to be a better way.*"

   You can also be that voice.

Final Advice: Keep Learning

The cloud never stands still. Neither should you.

Continue growing by:

- Earning advanced certifications like AWS Certified Cloud Financial Management and GCP Cost Optimization
- Joining the FinOps Foundation and participating in working groups
- Reading whitepapers on AI cost governance, FOCUS™, and cloud sustainability

- Experimenting with tools like Cloud Custodian, Prophet, and Open Policy Agent

Remember: *A certification might prove that you know the framework. However, it is your actions that determine its impact.*

Conclusion

FinOps is not just about saving money. It is about freeing resources for innovation, empowering teams with transparency, and building a sustainable, value-driven cloud future.

You now have the knowledge. The next step is leadership. Go make it happen.

Real-world FinOps adoption is not about achieving perfection from day one; it is about embracing continuous improvement, adaptability, and cross-functional collaboration. Every organization examined in this chapter faced unique challenges, but the most successful ones shared a common foundation of transparency, shared ownership, and a culture of learning.

Whether you are in a fast-moving startup or a global enterprise, FinOps provides a proven framework for achieving sustainable, value-driven cloud growth. By mastering core principles and staying ahead of emerging trends like AI cost governance and FOCUS™ for SaaS transparency, you position yourself not just as a cost manager, but as a strategic enabler of innovation.

And that is the heart of FinOps: aligning cloud spending with business outcomes, empowering teams with data, and turning financial accountability into a competitive advantage.

This is more than a practice. It is a mindset. And you are now well-equipped to lead it.

Questions

1. What are the most common challenges organizations face when implementing FinOps?
2. How can executive sponsorship help accelerate FinOps adoption?
3. What role do engineers play in FinOps, and how can they be incentivized to participate?
4. How can FinOps principles be applied to AI and machine learning workloads?
5. What are the key benefits of adopting the FOCUS™ specification for SaaS cost transparency?

Multiple Choice Questions

1. Which of the following is NOT a core principle of FinOps?
   a. Collaboration
   b. Visibility
   c. Isolation
   d. Accountability
2. What is the primary purpose of a FinOps Center of Excellence (CoE)?
   a. To replace finance teams
   b. To centralize all cloud decisions
   c. To guide and scale FinOps practices across the organization
   d. To eliminate cloud costs entirely
3. What does FOCUS™ stand for?
   a. FinOps Open Source System
   b. FinOps Operations and Usage Specification
   c. FinOps Open Cost and Usage Specification
   d. FinOps Operational Cloud Unit Standard
4. Which of the following is a challenge specific to managing AI costs?
   a. Low compute requirements
   b. Stable usage patterns
   c. Difficulty measuring ROI
   d. Easy tagging and attribution
5. What is a common outcome of embedding FinOps early in a startup?
   a. Increased cloud waste
   b. Flat cloud costs despite growth
   c. Reduced developer productivity
   d. Over-reliance on finance teams

Answers

1. c
2. c
3. c
4. c
5. b

Index

A

B

C

D

E